The Chocolate

Side of Life

The Chocolate

Side of Life

Cindy Sigler Dagnan

www.covenantpublishing.com

P.O. Box 390 Webb City, Missouri 64870
Call toll free at 877.673.1015

Library of Congress Cataloging-in-Publication Data
Dagnan, Cindy Sigler, 1965-
  The chocolate side of life / Cindy Sigler Dagnan.
    p. cm.
Includes bibliographical references.
  ISBN 1-892435-28-4 (pbk.)
  1. Christian life—Meditations. I. Title.
    BV4501.3.D34 2003
    242—dc21
                          2003001343

Dedication

*For my Father God who so graciously
bestows generous measures
of chocolate upon my life
&
For Debbie, who has shared
so much chocolate with me;
She will read this book
and in the kindest of ways, say,
"I told you so!"
Mmmmrrr . . .*

Table of Contents

Acknowledgments

- Thank you to my mother who gave me my love of all things chocolate.
- To my book club gals and pals and my Bible Study group for praying that this piece of chocolate might be inspirational and that deadlines might be met. . . . They were!
- Thanks to Eric from the radio station KKOW who played the songs I needed to hear the moment I requested them.
- Thanks to mom, Greg, Sharris and Tammy for reading chapters and pointing out errors. Special thanks for Sharris' unexpected appearance on my doorstep bearing corrected chapters, frosted brownies and chocolate milk—it made my day!
- Thanks to Becky Freeman whose incredible encouragement makes me keep writing and whose work is a chocolate-covered inspiration.
- Thanks to Steve and John at Covenant Publishing . . . they know how to bribe a gal with chocolate when they want a contract signed.
- Thanks to my four precious pieces of milk chocolate: Eden, Emmy, Ellie and Elexa. Thanks for all the days you played so nicely together so mommy could write. Let's celebrate with chocolate!
- Thanks to my husband, my friend and the love of my life. Without your support there wouldn't be this ending to my dark chocolate stories. I will never forget.

Compiled from
Family Circle, 1/2/01, 54
& *Redbook*, 6/01, 40

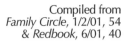

Chocolate Indulgences for Around a Mere 100 Calories...

1 packet instant hot chocolate mix w/ hot water
110 calories

4 chocolate candy kisses
100 calories

20 Goobers
104 calories

1/2 cup chocolate pudding
150 calories

9 small York Peppermint Patties
90 calories

Two Celebrations Mini candy bars
76 calories

A Fudgesicle
60 calories

10 chocolate covered raisins
41 calories

1/2 cup Ben & Jerry's Chocolate Fudge Brownie Frozen Yogurt
190 calories

Four chocolate-dipped strawberries
140 calories

Two Oreo cookies
107 calories

Chapter 1
The Case for Chocolate Living

"If some great catastrophe is not announced every morning, we feel a certain void. 'Nothing in the paper today,' we sigh."
—Paul Valery

Personally, I am so enchanted with chocolate that I have to agree with Erma Bombeck when she wrote this prayer, "Lord, if you can't make me thin, at least make my friends look fat!" Yep. Women everywhere seem to adore chocolate. Oh, we swap car trip tips, childbirth stories, recipes and secrets, but chocolate, now that's bonding!

We're all familiar with the famous Forrest Gump quote: "My mama told me that life is like a box of chocolates. You never know what you're going to get." Ain't that the truth?! Think back to the last time that you had your hands on one of those gourmet sampler boxes of chocolate. If you're honest, you can remember (especially as a child) taking tiny bites out of each piece, or puncturing the bottom of a promising piece with a fingernail, hoping for a caramel or a nougat filled chocolate, secretly groaning if you turned up coconut. Or worse yet, that gummy apricot filling. (Toffee never counted; its hard texture and square shape gave it away immediately.)

When it comes to chocolate, most of us would like to know in advance what we're going to select. A hot fudge malt. A Snickers Bar. A triple chocolate mocha. We tend to think of chocolate as the good stuff of life. The big trials, the tiny tumbles, the everyday annoyances cannot be chocolate. But that same suspended quality of never knowing what your teeth or fingernails are going to encounter, also makes life, like chocolate, such an adventure! I'd like to submit that all of life is chocolate – it's just a matter of perspective. Read on.

I read a lot about stress. For one thing, I can't help it. Every month, magazine headers trumpet the cures for my every ill: *231 Ways to Lead the Simple Life* (if my life was simple enough that I had time to finish that article, I wouldn't need it!); *12 Easy Steps to Conquering Clutter; Start Living Stress-Free Today!; Take Our Stress-O-Meter Test*

[I was off the charts!] I have tried all the plans with varying degrees of success. Okay, okay. With almost no success.

There is no end to my gullibility. Just the other day I was reading an article that listed some of the main symptoms of stress. Sleeping too much. Impulse spending. Excessive shopping. Eating indulgently. Driving too fast. *Are they kidding?!* I thought. *That's my idea of a perfect day!*

But seriously, our lives can't help being affected by our surroundings. By our mates. Our children. Our friendships. Our jobs. By our circumstances. Our God. In short, our lives are affected by life. *Life happens.*

Since this is true, I came up with my own plan—to delve into life wholeheartedly, enjoying each chocolate-filled moment along the way. To create and enjoy *the chocolate side of life*. Circumstances may affect us, but they don't have to finish us off. Take a deep breath, sit down on the couch, put your feet up and let's open the box of chocolates we call life together. I promise we'll find a piece you'll just love!

Take this quick test to evaluate your need for chocolate.

The last time I tried to find President Truman's nose in the clouds was:
    a) last year   b) last week   c) never
The last time I stopped at a child's roadside stand to buy lemonade was:
    a) last year   b) last week   c) never
The last occasion I had time to shave my legs (both of them) and wash my hair on the same day was:
    a) last year   b) last week   c) not since the children were born
The last time a saw a movie before it got to the dollar theatre or the video store was:
    a) last year   b) last week   c) when Reagan was President
The last time I finished my dinner while it was still hot was:
    a) last month
    b) last week
    c) I'm planning to when my youngest child leaves for college

---

Scoring:
• If you scored mostly A's, give yourself 6 M & Ms.
• If you circled mostly B's, go to the convenience store and splurge on a Snickers bar.
• If you circled mostly C's, go to Sam's Club and buy a case of Brach's double-dipped peanuts immediately.

Okay, now that we've evaluated your certifiable need for chocolate, let's get on with chocolate living! For starters, magazines have now been giving us headlines we chocoholics can celebrate:

- Health News: Chocolate can help you live longer! (*Woman's World* cover)
- Chocolate contains magnesium, which is part of bone & helps maintain calcium levels.
- Chocolate (and products containing chocolate) makes a substantial contribution to our copper intake, a mineral that aids in the prevention of anemia, and possibly, heart disease and cancer (*Good Housekeeping*, February, 2000, 138).
- Flavonoids in chocolate can lower bad cholesterol & fight build-up of artery clogging plaque.
- Moderately indulging in the chocolate you're craving may actually help you avoid an eating binge.
- Chocolate is not a culprit as a trigger for acne or migraine headaches!

But even better than the obvious health benefits of actually consuming chocolate, are the very real benefits to searching out the chocolate side of life. Living in the moment. Recognizing that although often the milk chocolate and dark chocolate moments are intermingled and life becomes bittersweet, it is *still* chocolate. Will Rogers with his wry humor once said, "Everything is funny as long as it's happening to somebody else." That may be true, but oh the power and joy of looking for the funny side of life's hard moments.

Ever wonder what a positive, joyful outlook could do for your life? Charles Swindoll, author and former pastor in a prominent California church shared this illustration from the pulpit one Sunday morning.

A single woman in her late twenties became very concerned that she was not yet married. In fact, she didn't feel that she had any decent prospects. So she began hanging a pair of men's pants over her footboard each night and praying this prayer:

Father in heaven, hear my prayer and grant it if you can;
I've hung a pair of trousers here, please fill them with a man.

Six months later she was married.

Soon after that Sunday illustration, a woman called Pastor Swindoll at his church office. Had she missed anything in the sermon that she needed to know about? "I'm not sure what you mean," he replied. "Well," she explained awkwardly, "it's just that my teen-aged son has been hanging a bikini over the foot of his bed. He said he learned it at church."

Ah, the optimism of youth! We chuckle at the story, but one thing remains true. For the Christian there is always hope and the assurance that God absolutely hears and answers our prayers. On sunny, milk chocolate days and dark ones.

"Life is 10% what happens to you and 90% how you respond to it."
Anonymous

Gaining a Chocolate Perspective

1. James 1:17 says that "Every good and perfect gift is from above, coming down from the Father of the heavenly lights. . . ." Make a list of at least five of these "good and perfect gifts" in your life. Are there any of them that you have failed to appreciate lately? If so, which ones? Why?

2. The flip side of those good and perfect gifts is a hard fact of life. We experience trials. All of us. Read James 1:2-4. What two qualities does perseverance promise?

3. Think of a time that you've recently experienced a trial. Did you think of it as a joy? Why or why not? What might help you change your perspective the next time you face a difficult or annoying situation?

4. Read Psalm 29:2. What do you think it means to "worship the Lord in the splendor of his holiness?" Do you truly enjoy doing so? Why or Why not? When are you most likely to feel that real worship is indeed a milk chocolate privilege?

5. Many great heroes in the Bible had positive, joyful attitudes, even in the midst of trials. However, positive thinking alone is not enough to transform lives, as some modern religions would have us think. Why isn't it? Read Acts 4:12;James 2:26.

 **Bits of Chocolate for Personal Reflection**

1. When and how have you worshiped God this week?

2. Read the "Faith Chapter," Hebrews 11. Memorize verses 1 & 2. Describe the relationship between faith & hope. Which one is easier for you? Why?

1900
Hershey's chocolate bar invented

1912
Oreos on the market

1998
47% of the U.S. food dollar was spent away from home . . . wonder how much of that was on chocolate?!

"Lead your life like you won't be ashamed to sell the family parrot to the town gossip."

Chapter 2
Defining Types of Chocolate

*"What a wonderful life I've had . . .
I only wish I'd realized it sooner."*

–Colette

Although it's my premise that all of life can be chocolate, there are definitely different types. For clarity's sake, I'll call the pleasant things in life "milk chocolate," and the hard times, "dark chocolate." [If you have chocolate dyslexia, you can just reverse these!] Peel off the wrapper and peek into this box of chocolates with me and let's explore all that the chocolate side of life has to offer.

MILK CHOCOLATE

Light, creamy, fluffy, and dreamy. This is the stuff good advertisements and great snacks are made of! It's comfort food. Milk chocolate is good for congratulations, thank-yous, and for mourning the little stuff like: your first or your fiftieth gray hair (who's counting?); PMS; a real or imagined slight; those five extra post-Thanksgiving pounds; the third time you took your driver's test; the day you seriously considered taking out an ad in the Sunday paper advertising a three for one special on your children . . . the list could go on and on!

Milk chocolate is being creative, hopeful, inventive, and optimistic. It's changing your perspective. Milk chocolate people stuff their chocolate boxes full of humor and unique outlooks. They are the types who make witty lists of ways to handle stress. I found these hilarious examples on the Internet.

- Make a list of things to do that you've already done.
- Put your toddler's clothes on backward and send him off to pre-school as if nothing was wrong.
- Retaliate for tax woes by filling our your tax forms with Roman numerals.
- Leaf through a *National Geographic* magazine and draw underwear on the natives.
- Pay your electric bill in pennies.
- In a restaurant, stare at people through the tines of a fork and

pretend they're in jail.
- Sit in a parked car with your sunglasses on and point a hair dryer at passing cars; see if they slow down.
- When the money comes out of the ATM, scream, "I won! I won! Third time this week!"

In a similar vein, one wit came up with things to do to occupy your time while waiting for your spouse in Wal-Mart.

- Walk up to an employee and say very seriously, "There's a code 57 in housewares."
- Go into a dressing room and say loudly, "Hey! You're out of toilet paper in here!"
- Challenge someone in the gift-wrap aisle to a duel with wrapping paper tubes.
- Arrange all the candy bags in order from most to least calories.

Single people who know the joy of chocolate living offer outrageous strategies for meeting new people:

- Stage a multicar accident, which allows you to get names and addresses of people you might never meet otherwise.
- Go to the airport arrival area and hold up a sign reading SMITH for deplaning passengers to read.
- Train your dog to run to attractive strangers (it worked in 101 Dalmatians).
- Take a Twister board to a doctor's waiting room.
- Go to a bus station and shout, "Would anyone here like to be the beneficiary of my life insurance policy?"

Nolan & Eve Sarrett, *I'm So Tired of Other People,
I'm Dating Myself* (Nashville: Thomas Nelson, 1993)

People who appreciate milk chocolate have confidence and a pocketful of snappy comebacks to the "I'm Breaking Up With You" scenario. Like what, you ask?

- Can I put you on hold for a second?
- What a relief! I've been meaning to say the same thing to you!
- And you are . . .?
- Can I have some money?

- You'll regret this. Maybe not today, maybe not tomorrow. But soon and for the rest of your stinking life.
- I want you to know that your little tax secrets are safe with me.

"The Heartbreak Handbook," in *The St. Louis Post-Dispatch* (December 30, 1993)

Milk chocolate lovers deliberately look for the fun in life. They seek out silliness. They look for bloopers in church bulletins. These are my favorites:

Scouts are saving aluminum cans, bottles and other items to be recycled. Proceeds will be used to cripple children.

The ladies Bible study will be held Thursday morning at 10. All ladies are invited to lunch in the Fellowship Hall after the B.S. is done.

Remember in prayer the many who are sick of our church and community.

A songfest was hell at the Methodist Church Wednesday.

The Little Mother's Club will meet Tuesday at 7:00p.m. Anyone wishing to become a little mother should meet the pastor in his study by Monday.

And on a church sign during the minister's illness:

God is good. Dr. Hargreaves is better.

Living the chocolate side of life means looking up. Taking time for the little things. Lingering for a visit. Taking a drive with no specific destination in mind. Lounging in your jammies. Savoring the first moments of a new day. Rocking the baby for ten extra minutes. Taking a nap with your toddler. Swinging on a porch swing. Sliding down a slide. Enjoying the feel of the crisp glossy pages of a new magazine, straight from the mailbox. Preferably a favorite, from which no one has yet cut the backs out of the articles you're dying to read for a school project. The creaminess of an ice cream cone (chocolate, of course). Sharing a secret and keeping one. Holding the hand of your mate as you drift off to sleep.

Milk chocolate involves rearranging your perspective, being inventive and hopefully optimistic. Like the man who once went to an insurance agent to fill out an application for life insurance. He answered the usual questions. Age. Height. Weight. Profession. Non-smoker.

Then came the final questions. Are your parents still living? *No.* Father's age at death. *45.* Cause of death? *Heart attack.* Mother's age at death. *56.* Cause of death? *Liver failure.*

The agent reviewed the man's application and said, "I'm sorry, but we just can't insure you. These are terrible answers!"

He got the same response at the next insurance place. At the third office, the agent said, "Sir, we could insure you, but you wouldn't be able to afford the premiums!"

There was only one more insurance office left in town, so the man decided he'd need to fudge a bit on the answers. This time his answers to the final questions were quite different.

Are your parents still living? *No.* Father's age at death. *82.* Cause of death? *Hit by a car while jogging.* Mother's age at death? *93.* Cause of death? *Childbirth.*

Milk chocolate moments are the joys of life. We need them. We crave them. Author and minister Chuck Swindoll has said that one of the greatest needs in today's society is the *return of joy.* Surveys taken after the September 11, 2001 tragedy reaffirm this need. We live in a world more in need of faith and joy than ever before.

Those with experience tell us that milk chocolate is an indispensable part of life. An anonymous friar in a Nebraska Monastery wrote these words:

> *If I had to live life over again, I would relax more.*
> *I'd make more mistakes and laugh lots.*
> *I would limber up, I would be sillier than I have been this trip . . .*
> *I would take more trips. I would be crazier . . .*
> *(I would) watch more sunsets. I would do more walking*
> *and looking. I would eat more ice cream and less beans.*
> *I would ride on more merry-go-rounds. I'd pick more daisies.*

Milk chocolate, then, is at once ascribing significance to everyday things, while being able to take yourself lightly. Thankfully, God has given me sooo many opportunities to laugh at myself and make others laugh, too. And I started early.

During my junior year of high school, one of my good friends was deaf. I watched him struggle with boredom during the church service. He could hear nothing, lip reading was too exhausting, and he refused to use sign language. He did not want to appear different. I coaxed him to study signing by promising that I would learn too. It was the beginning of a ministry to about ten deaf people in our congregation.

After a few months of classes at a local college, I was turned loose, interpreting the announcements and the song service every Sunday morning. One Sunday, fingers flying through an announcement, I looked up to find the entire row of deaf parishioners guffawing.

The announcement had been: *The singles group had a great time at the singles retreat last weekend.* I had inadvertently mixed up two signs. I had translated the announcement like this: *The singles group had a great time at the sex retreat last weekend!*

My father, who was the preacher, looked curiously over at the lot of us. "Do you want to share the laugh with the rest of the congregation?" Red-faced I shook my head. I most emphatically did not.

When I was doing my student teaching, I was determined to do things perfectly. My classroom would be a place of order, and my students would be as thrilled about American History as I was. All went well until the day of the tornado drill. I led my students out into the hallway in two neat lines. I efficiently directed them to face the wall, kneel down and cover their heads with their hands.

Moments passed and I could see commotion as the other teachers led their students down the stairwells. *Hmm,* I thought, *we must be the only class using this hallway.* I congratulated myself on my students' behavior. Moments later, smugness gave way to mortification. I had confused the short blast for a *tornado* drill with the longer *fire* drill signal and all of my students would have been little burnt balls like so many marshmallows at a campfire gone bad, had this been an actual fire.

As the fire chief made his way to my end of the hall, checking the building, his eyebrows shot up to his hairline. I mumbled something about incompetent substitutes these days and walked away. Those students never let me forget and every year that I teach, there's always someone around who repeats the story and lines everyone up against the wall!

Milk chocolate is delight. The ending of an excellent novel. The clarity and action of the big screen showing a marvelous movie. A baby's first belly laugh or toothless grin. An unexpected letter from an old friend. First loves.

Milk chocolate also contains a definite pleasure factor. Hot cocoa during a snowfall. A roaring fire. Trading confidences. Warm embraces. Bike riding with the wind in your face. Sunday drives. Even better, Sunday naps. Real popcorn with chocolate pieces mixed in. (I highly recommend buttered popcorn with Cookie Dough Bites candy.) Surprises. Beautifully wrapped packages. Fresh flowers. The sound of rain.

Perhaps most of all, milk chocolate invites laughter. Author and speaker Barbara Johnson tells my all-time favorite gut-busting story in her book, *Hanging Somewhere Between Estrogen and Death.*

A woman in mid-life became concerned about her aging mother. "Mom, you really should go to the doctor. I know it's unpleasant, but you can't keep putting it off. Why don't you come spend the night at my house. We'll watch movies, paint our nails, take bubble baths and make a girl's night out of it. Then I'll drive you to your appointment and take you out to lunch afterward."

Her mother agreed and the plans were made.

The next afternoon, over a sumptuous lunch, the mother and daughter visited.

"I'm puzzled about something," the mother frowned. "When the doctor was examining me this morning, he kept muttering, 'My, my aren't you fancy!' I can't think what he could be talking about. I just put on my plain white cotton panties this morning."

"Mom," the daughter put her hand on her mother's arm. "Did you use anything else besides the lotion and bath beads I put out for you this morning?"

"Well, no. Just some of that feminine deodorant spray that was under the cabinet."

The daughter groaned. "Mom! That wasn't deodorant, that was gold glitter hairspray!"

DARK CHOCOLATE

It's bittersweet. It has an edge. And if you closed your eyes, bit into it, and it wasn't what you were expecting, then . . . shudder. It might be filled with chopped nuts. Or coconut. Gag.

Dark chocolate hits when instead of "One of Those Days," we feel like we're having "One of Those Lifetimes!" We want to shout

LOUDLY, "Life's not fair!" and fall on our backs with a tantrum that'd put a two-year-old to shame. In a fit of pique, we find ourselves wanting to call every trucker's "1-800 How's My Driving" number with bad reports. As Barbara Johnson wrote in her book, *Splashes of Joy in the Cesspools of Life*, sometimes it seems that "the rain falls on the just and also on the unjust, but chiefly on the just, because the unjust keeps stealing the just's umbrella!"

How do we react to dark chocolate? What's the condition of our heart when someone steals our umbrella and the rain is pelting down? Some of us melt. Some of us discolor with bad attitudes. Nancy Reagan said that women are like tea bags. You never know how strong they are until you put them in hot water! Ouch. What a scalding truth!

And yet dark chocolate contains 25% pure chocolate, compared to milk chocolate's 15% (Susan Mitchell, *I'd Kill for a Cookie*). That means dark chocolate ends up with a more intense chocolate flavor. Maybe that in itself is a lesson about learning to enjoy dark chocolate.

Sometimes dark chocolate is merely the daily annoyances. Traffic jams. Telemarketers who call at dinner time. Time crunches. Killer deadlines. Bad-hair days. Bad-body days. Really rotten days.

Sometimes, you know it's gonna be one of those days. You can tell it's going to be a rotten day when

. . . You put your bra on backwards and it fits better.
. . . You turn on the news and they're showing emergency routes out of the city.
. . . Your twin sister forgot your birthday.
. . . The bird singing outside your window is a buzzard.
. . . Your pet rock snaps at you.
. . . Your car horn goes off accidentally and remains stuck as you follow a group of Hell's Angels on the freeway.
. . . You walk to work and find your dress is stuck in the back of your pantyhose.

– Source Unknown

Other times we drop our pieces of chocolate and they're crunched underfoot. Bitter filling comes pouring out. It sticks to the bottom of our shoe and smears our souls. We lose our life's mate to death or divorce. A child is born with a disability. We lose our job. A dear friend moves across the country . . . or across the world. We are diagnosed with a terminal illness.

We definitely prefer milk chocolate. It is tasty. It is easy to eat. It is frothy, but it does not build character. It makes up much of life, but it is not all there is. Sometimes, the milk and dark chocolate merge and life becomes bittersweet.

Bittersweet days make the milk chocolate days all the richer. When we recognize this, it changes our perspective. "Never regret. If it's good, it's wonderful. If it's bad, it's experience," wrote author Victoria Holt.

Often it seems that we pray more on dark chocolate days. I once read an anonymous author's words on surrender. "What men usually ask of God when they pray is that two and two not make four." If our most fervent prayers are on such days, perhaps we should pray with hearts of gratitude more often.

Our reaction to the dark chocolate days and moments of life is an uncannily accurate barometer of our attitudes and our character. Embracing the chocolate side of life means learning to accept both kinds with different styles, but equal grace.

"Your worst days are never so bad that you are beyond the reach of God's grace. And your best days are never so good that you are beyond the need of God's grace."

Anonymous

Gaining a Chocolate Perspective

1. Hebrews 12:11. Even though we know discipline is a necessary, even good, thing, why do we find it so unpleasant?

2. Read 2 Timothy 2:11-13. What three promises are there? Which one is your favorite? Why?

3. First Timothy 6:17 exhorts us to put our hope in God "who richly provides us with everything for our enjoyment." In what ways is this true of your life right now? Are there times when you doubt this?

4. No matter what is going on in your life right now, Proverbs 15:29 contains the biggest blessing of our prayer life. What does the writer mean by someone "righteous"? Do you have trouble praying when you feel you don't qualify?

Bits of Chocolate for Personal Reflection

1. Proverbs 13:19 says, "A longing fulfilled is sweet to the soul." What is your usual response during the waiting period for a "longing fulfilled"?

2. Why do we tend to question God during the hard times, yet rarely question, "What have I ever done to deserve all these blessings?"

Chocolate is the Number One food craved by women.

For men, pizza is the top pick.

Q: How many M&Ms are sold each day?   A: See Chapter 12

Americans consume about
3.2 billion pounds of chocolate per year.
That's 11.7 pounds per person and
more than $13 billion in retail sales!

Good Housekeeping,
February 2000, 134

Chapter 3
The Care & Keeping of Chocolate

"May your home be trimmed in love,
With joy wound 'round and 'round.
May laughter raise the rafters, And merriment abound. . .
May your hearth glow with the smiles of all your kith and kin,
And may heaven grace your humble place
As the good Lord dwells within.

—Irish House Blessing

During World War II, chocolate bars were placed into field knapsacks as part of the Allied Armed Forces' daily rations. Even today chocolate is still included in United States Army field rations. Chocolate bars have even accompanied our astronauts into space.

Chocolate has a definite place in history, and we women are among the best consumers. You can buy chocolate calendars, framed photographs of chocolate confections, chocolate shaped cabinet pulls, scented stickers, book marks, mousepads, books, T-shirts, stationery (scratch & sniff, of course!) candles, soaps and cards. There are even whole stores devoted to such decadence. On my last visit to a book superstore, I noticed that *The Art of Chocolate, I Love Chocolate* and *The Ultimate Chocolate Cookbook* were way outselling *Quick & Healthy Fat Free Cooking.* Indeed, chocolate has inspired both novels and ice-cream parlors entitled, "Death by Chocolate!" I say what a way to go! Not to be outdone, the Internet is getting in on the act. There is one Web site devoted to the subject: "Virtual Chocolate: Mouthwatering Images of Fabulous Treats!" And calorie-free.

I love how the precious woman at our favorite donut shop puts it: "Sweetheart, these donuts are calorie free, fat free and sugar free, because we don't charge extra for those things!"

CHOCOLATE RULES! SO HERE ARE SOME CHOCOLATE RULES
- Put "eat chocolate" at the top of your "to do" list each day. That way you'll get at least one thing done!
- Equal amounts of milk chocolate and white chocolate equal a balanced diet.
- Chocolate covered raisins, cherries, orange slices and dipped

strawberries count as fruit. Eat as many pieces as you like.
- A box of chocolates can provide your total daily intake of calories all in one place. Isn't that handy?
- Milk chocolate contains calcium, therefore it can be included in the dairy group.
- Calories in chocolate shared with a friend don't count.
- The problem: How to get 2 pounds of chocolate home from the store without it melting in the car. The solution: Eat it in the parking lot.
- If calories are an issue for you, store your chocolate on top of the refrigerator. Calories are afraid of heights, so they will jump out of the chocolate to protect themselves.

–Internet, source unknown

Chocolate is delightful. One of my favorite excursions is to a local chocolate shop called Richardson's Candy House. To walk in there is to get a step closer to heaven! They make maltballs from scratch! Hand-dipped strawberries. Double-dunked cashews and peanuts. A variety of shapes of chocolate suckers. Gold-wrapped chocolate coins. Usually transporting it isn't a problem; we devour our selections on the way home. [This is second only to a visit to Shake's Frozen Custard for a hot fudge malt. During my pregnancy with Emily, I had one every week. No osteoporosis for my baby, no siree!]

But chocolate is also fragile, I've learned. You can't leave it in your car on a hot day. Just ask my friend Lori who recently blew some serious bucks at a Godiva shoppe while on vacation. She saved part of a box of truffles to take home. Enroute, they stopped in St. Louis at Grant's Farm. In their eagerness to show their daughter the delights of the petting zoo, the entire family walked off and left the chocolate sitting in a bag! Alas it was July. When they returned to the car having completed the tourist thing, the chocolate was stuck to the inside of the bag, oozing out of the box corners, inedible. I nearly wept for her as she shared her tale. "I've only had Godiva truffles once. After Eden's birth my mother bought them for me as a reward for thirty-two hours of labor. Oh, Lori. I feel your pain."

There are other places you can't leave it either. You can't leave it unattended if your husband or children are around. My children can smell chocolate on my breath from eight feet away. They've been able to do this since nine months of age. I have to be careful about tucking them in at night if I don't have anything to share. And who can't relate to the commercial where the woman reaches for her secret stash of chocolate Pepperidge Farm cookies and finds them missing?

And sometimes vice versa. Not too long ago I brought my husband a white chocolate dipped Zero bar as a little perk. It's his favorite. "No reason," I smiled. "Just because I love you." I handed it to him and sat down by him, wolfing down my own Snickers bar. For some odd reason, he put his candy on the nightstand next to our bed.

The next morning as I got up and made our bed, I noticed it still lying there. I averted my eyes. *The candy is his. You cannot eat it, you bought for him.* I went to bed the following night, observing the candy, still untouched. I marveled at his self-control. When I awakened the next morning it was still there. I made the bed again. I answered a few letters at the little desk in my bedroom. I left the room to wash my face. I could hear the candy bar, calling my name.

A few days later, my husband got home from a grueling day at the office. At the end of the evening, I sat down next to him and noticed his eyes look longingly at the nightstand. "Cinso," he began sweetly, "I came home looking for my candy bar. I thought about it all day and figured it would hit the spot tonight. Any ideas where it could be?" I hung my head.

Then I blew it by blurting out, "Honey! I ate it! How much self-control do you think I have?!"

I did feel some remorse, but you have to understand, I married a man for whom chocolate is sometimes optional, if you can believe it. Last month I had the incredible adventure of shopping for groceries at Wal-Mart. Late at night. Alone. I had fun.

I also purchased something I'd never purchased before: Chocolate Decadence Cheesecake Bars. I had a coupon and decided that I simply could not pass them up. Back in the car, I nestled them in the front seat next to me and ate one while I waited for the traffic light to turn green. Yum.

They occupied my thoughts the rest of the six miles home. I unloaded the groceries and taped the box shut so nobody would notice they'd been opened. My husband helped me put the groceries away. The kitchen was clean. The children were in bed. I couldn't wait to share this treat with my husband.

"Sweetheart," my voice rang out in a sing-song voice. "I have a surprise for you. You'll really like it!" He turned a devastatingly handsome grin my way.

"No, silly, it's not that! It's almost better than that!"

He looked puzzled. "Like what?"

I smiled my brightest smile. "Chocolate Decadence Cheesecake Bars. Do you want one?"

He considered this for a moment. "No thanks," he said cheerfully and sauntered off.

No thanks? *No thanks?* What kind of man had I married?!

Aghast, I followed him up the stairs. "Why not?"

"I just wasn't in the mood for chocolate."

Who knew you had to be in a "mood" for chocolate?

Bars of chocolate in the bottom of your purse aren't a good idea either. The paper gets torn and disgusting bits of that bottom-of-your-purse gunk sticks to it. And mailing it makes it particularly vulnerable. You have to wrap it in bubble wrap and make sure the temperature is controlled.

Sometimes our very selves are fragile things too. Malleable and moldable, like chocolate. As women, we are born nurturers. We want to fix things, to be there for people. We fall into the superwoman trap. We squeeze every available moment of our days full. We wake up and hit the ground running. Readying the children for the day. Slapping lunches into paper sacks. Warming Pop Tarts. Hunting for lost things.

We want to send our spouses off to work with a cheerful heart. We'd like to do devotions and we feel guilty about skipping exercise again. Whether we work in the home or out of it, something or someone pulls energy from us the entire day. At the end of it there is dinner to prepare. A table to clear. Dishes to wash. Homework to do. Housework to do. Children to bathe. Preparations for tomorrow. Bills to pay. Friends who call, needing us. And, oh yeah, we really should take some time out that is special and meaningful for our spouse. Whew! It's exhausting. And if there is any spare time we all too often feel guilty about claiming for ourselves. So we skulk to a corner chair and attempt to read a bit of a book, a snippet of a magazine article.

We are experts at taking care of others, but we often neglect ourselves. Stealing chocolate moments of solitude and refreshment is truly an investment in our own health and energy, allowing us better returns for all the relationships we hold dear.

Sometimes we even care too much what people think. When I quit teaching school full-time in order to have more time with my children, public perception of me changed somewhat. Some of it was favorable: *That's great! You'll never have these years back.* Some of it was not. *Are you nuts?! You just finished your Master's degree. What a waste!* It took a while for me to behave as confidently in my decision as I felt. I hadn't realized my self-worth was so linked to what I do.

Some of the changes have gotten me into a lot of trouble. Not wanting to allow my relationship with my husband to go stale, I have done a lot of things that turned out to be, well, embarrassing. One day, hoping to enliven the dull routine of working all day and remodeling our ancient farmhouse all night, I called my husband's private line at work. When he picked up the phone, I put on my very best sultry voice. "Hey, baby," I drawled. "Wanna come home and paint the bedroom naked?"

"Well, sure," laughed the voice on the other end of the line. "I'm just not sure my *wife* would like that very much!" The voice belonged to the County Prosecuting Attorney! My husband's boss. It was a while before I dared show my face in that office. Now when he introduces me to people, he says, "This is Greg's wife. She's an author and a painter."

You'd have thought I'd learned my lesson. Not so. A few months ago, I was reading a magazine article about not taking your man for granted. So I began a mail campaign. The first day I mailed my husband a letter thanking him for all the qualities I appreciated about him. The second day I sent him a work-related cartoon. The third day I posted a book about fathering he'd been wanting. And the fourth? I went all out – I mailed him the Hot Monogamy sex tip from *Ladies' Home Journal.* I topped with a very personal Post-It, anticipating a volcanic response.

I got more than I bargained for. That night my husband came home and said, "Cinso, we need to talk. I really appreciate the sentiment behind all the things you've been sending me and I'm sure the secretaries enjoy reading all your notes too."

I gulped. "Whaaat?! I thought mail was private!"

"Not in our office. We get so many hateful letters from bad guys that we have an open-mail policy. That way only the important stuff gets left on our desk every morning."

"This is important," I squeaked.

Then he saw my face. "What did you send today?"

My heart raced and I hung my head. "I don't want to tell you. It'll ruin the surprise. But *please* make sure you get to the mail bag before they do the next two days."

The next day I got a phone call. "How badly do you want a story for your next book?"

I groaned. "You didn't make it!"

He laughed, "Nope. But I sure am getting some looks of respect around here!"

Even my view of myself changed somewhat. I could no longer look at a "To Do List" filled with red lines signifying accomplishment to define what I did during my days. I was busier than ever, but I couldn't always pinpoint exactly what I'd done.

During this time Eden brought home her Social Studies book. Leafing through it I saw a painting by August Renoir entitled "Woman With Cat." I began to imagine him painting scenes from my current life. "Exhausted Woman With Snotty Knees, Baby Food Shoulders, Three Clinging Kids, Two Cats, Six Chickens and One Dog"; "Woman Buys Mop"; "Woman With Mop"; "Woman As Mop." I quickly concluded there wouldn't be much of a market for any of those.

Indeed life is richer, fuller, but vastly different. A friend sent me a Hallmark *Shoebox* card. On the front is a lady in a pristine 1950s housedress folding laundry. A caption near her mouth says, "Sometimes I think about chucking it all to become a supermodel . . ." The inside reads, "Then I laugh real hard and go back to sorting socks!" That, in a nutshell, summed up my life.

Some of the changes were just frustrating. Suddenly, everyone began to think of my time as his or her own. I was asked to serve on every committee and volunteer for every bake sale. People wanted me to watch their children, walk their dogs and pull their weeds. Learning to say no was a difficult and new skill for me.

I learned that in order to have time for chocolate, precious areas of your life must be savored and stored.

Life, all of it, is a gift. But especially those tantalizing, taste-bud-teasing moments of milk chocolate. They come along more often than you'd think. If you just know where to look and how to keep them once they're found.

 ### Gaining a Chocolate Perspective

1. Psalm 119:82 asks, "When will you comfort me?" Verse 94 entreats, "Save me, for I am yours." We are on dangerous ground when we turn to anything other than God for comfort, even chocolate. What kinds of things do you turn to for comfort?

2. Proverbs 10:24 says that "what the righteous desire will be grant-ed." Do you ever have trouble believing that? What evidence have you seen that it is true?

3. Read Proverbs 4:23. How does the admonition to guard your heart apply to the "care and keeping of chocolate"? Of what things do you need to take better care? What burdens might need to be stored away in the depths of God's forgiveness?

4. Proverbs 24:10 admonishes, "If you falter in times of trouble, how small is your strength!" Why is it so hard to have the proper outlook during hard times? Think beyond the obvious.

 Bits of Chocolate for Personal Reflection

1. In what areas of your life are you the most malleable and ready for God to work? In what areas of your life are you most fragile and vulnerable?

2. "Does not he who guards your life know it?" (Proverbs 24:12). In what ways is this verse disturbing? Comforting?

If you're a cola drinker, nearly 10 pounds per year can be effortlessly dropped by exchanging it for water or a diet version. I learned in math class that drinking a Diet Coke with a Snickers cancels out the calories, as a positive and negative cancel each other out! :)

The caffeine contained in an ounce of milk chocolate is about the same as a cup of decaffeinated coffee.

Sweet Chocolate Dates...

February 14
VALENTINE'S DAY

April 28
KISS YOUR MATE DAY

August
ROMANCE AWARENESS MONTH

Chapter 4

The Milky Way & Hershey Kisses

"People who throw kisses are hopelessly lazy."
                                                    –Bob Hope

"Cinso," my tough, cop husband lamented. "Before this is all over, I'm going to be the one writing the books! You have complicated my life!"

"At work there are only three things you can do with the bad guys: arrest them, interrogate them, or let them go. With you, I have to figure out which of the 196 things you might be needing today!"

Sigh. It's true. I can't even get mad when my husband borrows a line from his favorite television cop to describe me: high maintenance like a broad! The age-old conflict of the fundamental differences between men and women is still going strong today. During the late 1990s, *Time* magazine belatedly made it a rather obvious headline: "Men & Women Are Different." Hmmmm. . . . For this they went to Journalism College? I think it probably began way back in the Garden of Eden.

"Honey," Eve called to Adam. "Do you like the large fig leaf best? Or do you think I'd look better stringing a batch of those gorgeous-colored autumn leaves together?"

"Look," Adam replied in a bored tone. "It doesn't make any difference to me. I think you look great in anything. Personally, I like you best au natural, the way you looked when I first saw you."

Eve probably huffed off in search of other options and a debate about whether gardenias or roses looked best in her hair.

Yep. It's an age-old conflict. As the saying goes, "When women are depressed, they either eat or go shopping. When men are depressed they invade another country. It's a whole different way of thinking."

The wonderful news about the blending of these differences into this thing called marriage is that it has the potential to generate pure bliss. The downside is, approximately thirty-seven hours after the honeymoon, we realize it takes hard work.

For women, this is particularly hard to take. We can become disillusioned because that knowledge is opposite of the way we were raised. Most of us consumed a steady diet of fairytales: in books, at the movies and Disney-style. All the heroines met and married handsome princes without so much as lifting a finger. (Well, except Snow White and she managed to get seven little men to help out.) The only couple I witnessed having any real degree of trouble was Belle and the Beast. (My husband said the Little Mermaid doesn't count on this front. Even though Ariel couldn't talk, the Prince was happy about that.) Snow White's and Sleeping Beauty's charmers knew not only where they could be found, but also exactly what they needed. And when Cinderella threw a shoe, did she have to dialogue with the Prince to tell him what the problem was? No way. Sit-coms don't count either. All problems are resolved within twenty-four minutes, allowing time for commercials. (Hey, there's an idea: take a commercial break during your next spat!)

In my opinion, this is the root of most marital discord: high expectations hover warmly and are slapped down when they meet the cold air of reality. Neither person's expectations are necessarily wrong, they're just different.

This is true even about simple issues. For example, if my husband is headed home from work after a particularly rotten day, his fondest expectation may be to sit down to a hot meal, a tall glass of iced tea and an evening of vegging in front of the TV. Understandable.

However, during that same day, perhaps I've developed a nearly incurable case of cabin fever. I am tired of the children. The dust bunnies no longer strike me as cute cheap pets. I've opened the kitchen pantry and experienced the same feeling I had when I opened the closet that morning: there's nothing to eat and I don't feel like cooking. Brilliant idea: *Let's all go out to eat! We haven't done that for a while. I can take the cost out of next week's groceries. Hurrah!* Also understandable.

I hear Greg's tires crunch on the gravel drive. I fly out the door to meet him, barely apologizing to the kitten, which has now involuntarily parachuted off the back steps. He alights from the car, shoulders drooping, and greets me with a kiss and a weary smile. *How nice to be home to stay.*

In my haste to get four children strapped into various kinds of car seats, booster seats and seatbelts, I miss this less-than-enthusiastic reaction to my plan. "What," I ask, "Are you not wanting to go out?"

Here two problems begin. First, there is that bothersome issue of two people's differing expectations. Second, there is a disparity in the way we communicate. Greg will say, "Oh, honey. It doesn't make any difference to me where we eat. You go ahead and pick."

"Noooo," my voice will flirt with whining. "It's not as much fun if you aren't involved. Just tell me what you really want to do."

Poor guy. No matter what he says next, it's a losing situation. He will either say, "Well, I've had a rough day. I'd just as soon stay home." Alternately, he will say (and actually mean!) "It really doesn't matter to me."

If he picks the former choice, it's likely that I will huff, "Well fine. Why didn't you say so in the first place. I knew you didn't want to go anywhere. Let's just stay here!" If he chooses the latter, I won't believe him. I'll pick the statement apart, looking for context clues as to his "real" meaning. Pure projection, since only about two out of every ten times that I say I have no preference is that really true.

That's the same reason that if Greg has hurt my feelings, I will resort to fairytale mode, expecting him to read my mind. I sit, hugging the passenger side of the car. After about ten minutes of attempted conversation with me, this man who is a crackerjack at solving murders and other crimes against persons, but can be mystified by his own wife, will finally realize that I'm not really holding up my end.

"Cinso? Is something bothering you?"

Big huffy breathing resonates from my side. "No. I'm fine. Thanks."

And because he is a man, he will say, cheerily, "Great!" and continue telling me about his day. Men are so literal.

My point is this. There is no "secret" to having a lasting, enduring, fulfilling marriage. All of them, even the great ones (no, especially the great ones) take work. The next time you see a magazine whose headline blares, "The One Secret You Must Know for Marital Bliss," read at your own risk.

That said, there are some practical principles and timely tips that I have filched, observed, and slogged through for making a marriage great. Here they are,

---

"The difference between courtship and marriage is the difference between the pictures in a seed catalogue and what comes up."

–James Wharton

THE TOP TEN LIST OF WHAT MAKES LOVE LAST

1. Recognition of the Sacredness of the Beginning Vow. Chances are when you repeated your vows with equal parts wonder, excitement, anticipation and trepidation, you were confident that you would always feel just as you did on your wedding day. No effort involved, just that glorious, "just swallowed a goldfish" fluttery, euphoric ever after. "For better or worse?" Can't be that hard. What could ever happen that would be "worse?"

My husband and I have a huge enlargement of our favorite wedding picture that hangs in our great room above the piano. Our smiles are glowing. He is unbearably handsome in his formal tuxedo. I am willowy and beaming in my flowing dress, carrying red tulips, shoes daintily buckled with pearl buttons. He is in the process of twirling me around. Snap! The photographer froze that moment in time forever.

Our job is to make sure the photographer didn't merely embalm that moment. Scripture tells us that it is better not to make a vow than to make a vow and not keep it. It also tells us that we are blessed when we keep a vow, even when it hurts. And sometimes it will. No matter, our sacred duty has not changed. It is holy. It is forever. God honors those who keep it.

2. Practice Candid & Careful Communication. At first glance, this seems both simple and cliched. Trust me, not so. If communication were simply talking, there'd be no problem. Or if we weren't both sometimes guilty of interchanging the meaning of sarcasm and candidness. Or if we both always heard what was meant or meant what we said or . . . as Mark Twain wrote, "The difference between the right word and the almost right word is the difference between lightning and a lightning bug!"

While dating, we wouldn't have dreamed of yawning during our future mate's discourse. Of interrupting with a "better" idea of our own. We chose our words carefully, desiring to be courteous and respectful.

And talk we did! Remember those dreamy days of courtship, when there never seemed to be enough time to share? Sitting on a couch, in a car, at a restaurant table, under the stars, on playground swings, on the porch steps—anywhere—talking. Sharing dreams, wedding plans and the deep gritty stuff of the soul.

The trick is to keep it up amidst the ordinary "dailyness" of life. Some things need to be said often. I love you. I'm sorry. I'll do that. How I appreciate you. However, as the witty Michelle Gelman said, "The difference between a successful marriage and a mediocre one consists of leaving about three things a day unsaid."

Remember to watch not only what you say, but also how you say it. Communication is 58% non-verbal, 35% tone of voice and only 7% your actual words.

After sharing with women (and men too) on the topic of marital conversation, I am often asked, "This is terrible to admit, but by the time we finally make all the arrangements to be alone, we don't have anything to talk about. How do we start?" You might try by pocketing one or two ideas that initiate deeper conversation.

CREATIVE CONVERSATION STARTERS FOR MARRIED COUPLES
- If you could keep only one memory, what would it be?
- What color was your day?
- If you suddenly inherited $500,000 what would you do with it first? After me, who would you tell about it first?
- Pick five adjectives to describe our sex life.
- What do you remember most fondly about the births of each of our children?
- If you had to switch careers now, what would you choose to become?
- What was your favorite food in the fourth grade?
- Who was your favorite teacher? Why?
- When you were ten, what did you plan to become when you grew up?
- If you could plan a family vacation to anywhere (money being no object) this year, where would you take us? On a couple's vacation?
- What is your favorite Scripture verse?
- When is it the hardest for you to pray? Why?
- If you could improve me in one area, what would that be?
- What new thing would you like to try in our sex lives?
- If our house was on fire and you had time to save only one possession (the rest of us being safe) what would you save?

Fighting, or as we call it in our house, "having a discussion," also needs to be addressed here. Heed Paul's warning in Ephesians 4:26, "Do not let the sun go down while you are still angry." In verse 27, he explains why: do not give the devil a foothold. Left unchecked, anger is a dangerous thing. Resentment accumulates quickly when you have periodic conversations with your pillow. *I can't believe he is being so insensitive! How can he not know he hurt my feelings?* Punch pillow. Sigh heavily. He just doesn't appreciate me. And the road, over time could grow more slippery. *I bet so and so wouldn't treat his wife that way. If I had married* _____ . . . ."

That kind of silent treatment encourages puffy eyelids and indigestion. How much better to reconcile and cuddle for the rest of the night. One man who had been married for over fifty years was once asked his secret for following this rule. "Simple," he replied, "We just stay up until I eventually agree with her! We've seen a lot of pretty sunrises!"

Learn not just to apologize, but also to ask forgiveness. I need to ask more often than I do. While I prefer to refer to my sarcastic tendencies as having a "caustic wit," I know that it can wound. In marriage we have a unique opportunity to forgive and enjoy forgiveness. Charles Caleb Colton put it this way: "Marriage is a feast where the grace is sometimes better than the dinner!"

3. Preservation of Oneness. Your relationship with your spouse is your most important EARTHLY priority. Guard your time. The demands of work, bills, children, church commitments, extended family, chores, hobbies and a fast growing lawn will all vie for your attention. So write in your date nights. Get away once a year; go out on a date once each month; have lunch together once a week, if possible; connect every day. Studies show that the first 7 seconds that we reconnect set the tone for the whole evening! Make them good ones.

Write down your time together on your calendar. Seem silly? Think about it. You write everything from soccer practice to dental appointments to sale days on your calendar. Is your marriage less important than those things? A written time also solidifies your commitment and prevents other things from swallowing it up.

If you suffer from mommy guilt, remember two things: your children will survive without you and someday they will grow up and leave. Leave them the legacy and the example of a strong marriage. Model one like they will want to choose one day.

Genesis 2:24 records some of the first words about this God-ordained relationship. "For this reason a man will leave his father and mother and be united to his wife, and they will become one flesh." If you truly learn to become one flesh, you will devote time to the health of that flesh and will be wary of causing your spouse pain.

4. Shared Experiences. Do things together. Share with each other the things that you read and the activities that you pursue separately. Girlfriends, it is important to remember that your husband's need for

Companionship is equal to your need for *Conversation*. Happy is the man whose wife will engage with him in the activities he enjoys (yes, that includes sex, but that's not all there is). No doubt during your courtship, you have been (or at least pretended to be) enthralled by sports, his taste in music and were generally game for whatever he had planned. Do it again.

When Caroline Kennedy was a little girl, one of the Sisters at her Catholic school asked the children to put their heads on the table and think about how Jesus loved them. After a few minutes, she asked them what the exercise made them think about.

Caroline raised her hand. "It made me think of how my mommy always watched cowboy movies with my daddy," she said, "because my daddy always liked cowboy movies. My mommy doesn't like cowboy movies at all, but she watched them because she loved my daddy" (Christopher Andersen, *The Day John Died*, 47, William Morrow Publ., 2000).

Love is like that. How long has it been since you've done something with your spouse that you don't particularly enjoy, just because you know they'd love sharing it with you?

Private jokes, the trials we have overcome, pleasant secrets, the way our eyes can lock over the dinner table or at a social gathering and communicate volumes are all experiences that bind Greg and me to each other. We know things, intimate things, silly things; painful things about each other that are for our eyes alone.

Each time you share something exclusively with your spouse, your relationship is all the more protected.

It is also important to support each other's dreams and endeavors. I could not do the writing or speaking that I do without Greg's whole-hearted backing. His response nearly any time I need him is "No problem." At least one evening each week he takes the little girls (all four of them!) out somewhere for an adventure so I can have an uninterrupted writing night.

A few weeks ago, he was sharing a few of his dreams with me and paid me the greatest compliment. "I'm not sure I would be attempting half of what I want to do without your support. Thank you for unfailingly believing in me."

5. A Sense of Humor. To laugh at yourself and with each other is a rich blessing. Laughter is an aphrodisiac, an age-reducer, stress-reducer, tummy tightener, day brightener and is much, much cheaper than therapy.

Look for the bright side of frustrating situations together. Deliberately seek out opportunities to laugh together. Rent old movies, or vintage television shows, pop some real buttered corn, pour Coca-Cola into a huge icy glass with two straws and curl up together.

Laugh even when times get tough. If they haven't already – don't worry – they will. As one unknown author wrote, "You can never tell about a marriage from the outside; some couples hold hands because they're afraid if they let go, they'd kill each other!"

6. A Sense of Fun. Play together. Board games. Question games. Tickle-fests. Of necessity, much that you do in marriage can be taking care of business. But don't ever squash the delights of spontaneous fun and a well-honed sense of the ridiculous. My husband absolutely cracks me up with his awful puns and crazy antics. He once pretended to dance for our washing machine because I had asked him "to turn it on." For my part, I absolutely relish the times I can make my husband laugh out loud. It is a sweet, chocolate sign that I can still get to the heart of what he needs.

One of my worst temptations is to fall in love with a specific time and place in our marriage and then spend all my energy trying to freeze it there. Not only is it not possible, it really isn't desirable. To attempt to make a still shot out of what is meant to be a motion picture invites stagnation. Learn new skills. Challenge your mind. Think outside the box.

"An archaeologist is the best husband any woman can have. The older she gets, the more he is interested in her!"
–Agatha Christie

7. Sizzling Sex. You knew that would be somewhere in this list, didn't you? What a mixed reaction I get when I speak about this to women's groups, or when my husband and I do marriage seminars or Valentine Banquets! Many times women will come up to me afterward, or write me and thank me for being so candid. Others will complain about having to "give in" to their husbands.

I think sometimes we've lost the thrill of sex or forgotten what a wonderful gift it is. We've also forgotten how vital an ingredient it is to a solid marriage. Zsa Zsa Gabor observed, "Husbands are like fires, they go out if unattended."

Kay Cole James, a wonderful Christian speaker and secretary of health under the Reagan/Bush administration, says, "Sister-girlfriends, the sad, sorry truth of it is, if you're not giving your husband what he needs [sexually] there are women out there who will!" She adds with much love and laughter, "We need to bless the brothers!"

Body image seems to be a big hurdle for women when it comes to sex, especially after bearing children. They think their thighs are too big. Their stretch marks are too, well, stretchy. Their breasts are too small. *Naked?!* They think, shrieking silently inside their heads, *What's wrong with just pulling up the flannel nightgown a tad?!*

Well, plenty. If you haven't caught on by now, guys are visual creatures. Just glimpsing a hint of skin while we put on our p.j.s before crawling into bed can turn them on. And if they glimpse cleavage, there'll be fireworks for sure! Remember the adage – women need a reason; men just need a place.

The good news is this. During an informal survey, I found out the secret "guy scoop" on what our husbands are thinking when they see us naked. Are you ready for this?

They are thinking "Wow! I am alone with a naked woman and she is going to let me have my way with her!!! Yowza! Yowza!"

Isn't that so comforting? They are not dissecting every flaw or mentally making a checklist of things we could change; they want us, in every sense of the word. You are the only person with whom your husband can purely and wonderfully quench such a powerful sexual thirst. With that confident mindset, get ready to bless!

- Try candlelight. Its romantic shimmer is flattering to every body.
- Bring fruit and chocolate dipping sauce into the bedroom. Take turns feeding each other.
- Try a new position and you be the one to initiate it.
- Read Song of Solomon aloud to each other.
- Buy something to wear in bedroom besides that holey gray T-shirt you usually wear.
- Play romantic music.
- Play strip poker.
- Make him a coupon booklet of fun favors for him to use whenever he desires.
- No matter how tired you feel, have sex every night for an entire week. You'll find that having sex begets the desire for more sex.
- Buy your husband a new tie and wear only that to bed.

- I once saw an ad, which read, "Every woman should own a dress that is capable of making a grown man cry." Go shopping, girlfriends!
- Make love in another room besides the bedroom. For that matter, make love in all the rooms!
- Wear a long strand of pearls and a pair of black pumps. Period.
- Skip the underwear underneath your dress. Just before you go out to dinner, tell him you "forgot."

Here's a fun side note. Sex is beneficial to your husband's health too! British researchers found that men can cut their risk of heart attacks in half by having sex two or more times a week (*Parents*, April, 2001, 95). Here's to healthy hearts!

8. A Sense of Romance. I know I'm probably preaching to the choir here, but we need to be reminded to bring beauty (I'm talking atmosphere here, those intangible and tangible qualities of our homes and our spirits that invite and welcome people to relax, unwind and be themselves) into our lives and our homes.

The results that little things can yield are inestimable:

- a single rose for her for no reason (men)
- a song dedication on the radio (either of you)
- a card and sexy pair of undies, spritzed with your perfume and placed in his suitcase when he leaves on a business trip to remind him what's waiting at home (ladies)

Does it take a little extra time and effort? Of course. But can you think of any investment that you'd want the return on if no one were willing to put any work into the company?

For any guys that may be reading this, you'll just have to trust me. Romantic gestures are as necessary to us women as air. Gary Smalley shares this story in his marriage seminars and it just slays me every time I hear it.

A husband became convicted that he needed to earnestly work on his marriage. He asked around and found that women love flowers, adore surprises and go batty over a well-chosen greeting card. One day he decided to take the plunge and begin his newly romantic behavior.

He came home from work early, bearing the most romantic Hallmark card he could find, a dozen pink roses, and a beautifully wrapped gift. Opening the door, he swept his startled wife off her feet. He was shocked to find that she was sobbing when he put her down.

"Honey," he pleaded, puzzled. "I thought you would like all this stuff! What's the matter?"

Between sobs, his wife managed to choke out, "I've had a terrible day! The kids were awful, the dishwasher broke, the washing machine overflowed, and now you come home drunk!!"

Guys, if you think this might be your wife's reaction, then it's been way too long!

9. A Sense of Wonder. The blending and uniting of two wills, two interests, two souls into one flesh, one body, one flesh is a phenomenal mystery. Two and yet one. The math may not add up, but the miracle of its truth of nothing short of lovely. Divine. To constantly be in the process of this "oneness" is a sacred privilege. We would do well never to lose this awe and wonder.

A farmer once came in from the pasture, his heavy work boots tracking in mud and clods of dirt all over her freshly scrubbed floor.

His wife's friend commented, "Those boots sure do bring in the mud! Isn't that aggravating?"

"Yes," the farmer's wife gently replied, "but they bring him in too." She knew the magic of wonder.

Every year on our anniversary, my husband and I make a point of watching our wedding ceremony video. We are once again caught up in those feelings, that anticipation, that newness. The habit of remembering translates into reliving that wonder in our every day lives.

10. The Glue of Commitment. Oh how I want a fiftieth wedding anniversary. I am so excited about it, that I want to invite you all in advance. How touchingly, achingly beautiful it is to see an older couple, gnarled hands, intertwined, obviously still in love.

My husband's parents went the distance—'til death do us part. They wanted that same solid relationship for their only son. My parents were married for 34 years, one month, eight hours and seventeen minutes. For their last anniversary they chose the same anniversary card. They were soul mates until cancer took him Home at age fifty-six. What a precious legacy they left to us, their children.

One of my other all-time favorite couples, Emmett and Vi Green, celebrated their fiftieth wedding anniversary a short four years ago. Just prior to his death, a few months ago, rapidly failing health put him in the hospital for an extended stay. He never got to go home. Vi kept long hours there. Exhausting hours. Tearful prayer-filled hours. We never arrived at the hospital for a visit that she was not beautifully put together. She was determined to be there for her husband in sickness and in health. Her commitment and great love for Emmett was obvious, even in this small attention to detail.

She and Emmett had been guest speakers at the local high school one spring. I had asked them to come and be part of a marriage panel, which I held for my Sociology students during our unit on marriage and the family. With trademark humor and dry candor, their quiet determined love story wrapped itself around the hearts of my students.

I know this for certain because one student wrote on her evaluation, "Mrs. D – The marriage panel was great! My mom has been married a bunch of times and none of them worked out. You're always talking about how wonderful committed marriage is, and how you should wait for that until sex, and stuff, but I thought you were crazy. To be honest, I figured I'd just live with someone since forever hasn't worked out in my family. After listening to [the Greens] I think I have changed my mind. They've been married over forty-five years and it's obvious they're happy."

Doug Larson put it this way, "More marriages might survive if the partners realized that sometimes the better comes after the worse." I love to ask people if I can look at their wedding pictures and hear the story of their courtship. They are usually happy to oblige and I learn much from their stories. Nearly every long-married couple echoes Mr. Larson's sentiment. *The longer we're married, the better it gets. Oh, we've had our share of problems, but if you stay with it, you'll find it's always sweeter on the other side.*

I believe them. I've seen it happen. I crave it for my own marriage. Marriage cannot succeed based on emotion. Sooner or later, you will wake up and for a brief period think, "I don't feel like being married today." It is then that you realize the purpose of commitment. Truly loving someone is a choice. It's an action word, a verb, rather than a flimsy, mushy noun.

Researchers asked the question "What does love mean?" to a group of 4 to 8 year olds. One little girl, Rebecca, 8, answered this way: "When my grandmother got arthritis, she couldn't bend over and paint her toenails anymore. So my grandfather does it for her all the time, even when his hands got arthritis too. That's love." I agree.

What does it matter if you live out your vow or not? It effects everyone who witnessed your vows, and a whole world that is watching. It effects your children. Judith Wallerstein, Ph.D. in her recent book, *The Unexpected Legacy of Divorce: A Landmark 25-year Study,* found that while children are resilient, they don't simply "bounce back" after experiencing parental splits. Wallerstein found that indeed they suffer most as adults as they try to form intimate relationships. And, God hates divorce.

Yes, there are provisions for divorce; I never wanted to be a part of them. But if I could reach anyone in the "I'm just not happy; bet I'd be happier with someone else" crowd, I'd remind them of their commitment, that even if the grass is greener, it still has to be mowed, and that sweet chocolate lives just around the corner from perseverance.

A few years ago, I heard two country songs back to back. They had to have been intended for my upcoming marriage seminar, because I only listen to the "twangier" stations when I'm forced to because no other broadcast frequency is available. I'm glad I did though, because they changed a significant part of my life.

One song is Chad Brock's "Ordinary Life." During the song, the dad ends up walking out on the family because he can't stand his ordinary life: paying bills, going to work, watching TV, going to church, fixing the leak, only to fix it again. He doesn't see magic in any of it. "I'm so sorry, bigger dreams are waiting for me – I can't do this anymore . . . I feel like I'm trapped inside this ordinary life."

His wife, Shelly, and their son go on with life. Shelly is grateful for crayons and her son at the kitchen table. Thankful for the ordinary routine; so thankful for every day. "Precious are the days as they go by, in their ordinary life."

At song's end, the husband and father calls home at midnight one night, full of regrets. What he wouldn't give to his ordinary life back. At what cost, that lesson?

The other song is a delightful take on the same experiences. It's entitled, "Just Another Day in Paradise," sung by Phil Vassar. Occasionally I'll call our local station and ask them to dedicate the song to my precious keeper of our home's paradise. Here's the opening stanza:

Phone Ringin', kids screamin',
dog barkin' at the mailman
bringin' up a stack of bills, overdue.
"Good morning baby, how are you?"

Throughout the song, various glitches in their day continue. *There goes the washing machine – baby don't kick it, promise I'll fix it with about a million other things. . . .* The couple attempts to have dinner out. Things happen, doesn't look like they'll make the dinner date, so they good humoredly go to Plan B. Domino's Pizza by candlelight. Then they'll make love that's "overdue." Wouldn't you know it. One of their children comes in the bedroom with his teddy bear. He's had a nightmare and wants to sleep in between them. Sound familiar?

Yet again comes the refrain.

> *Well it's okay, so nice,*
> *just another day in paradise.*
> *There's no place that I'd rather be.*
> *Two hearts, one dream,*
> *I wouldn't trade it for anything,*
> *and I ask the Lord, every night,*
> *for just another day in paradise.*

Oh, did you catch it? The difference a perspective makes. *You can have just an ordinary life or you can come home each night to nothing less than paradise.*

> Married people have the lowest rates of alcoholism,
> depression, and mental disorders when compared to unmarried,
> divorced, and separated individuals.
>
> Family Research Council, 2001

> *"What is better than a good woman? Nothing."*
> ───────────────────────────── –Geoffrey Chaucer

 ### Gaining a Chocolate Perspective

1. Read 1 Corinthians 13:4-13. What are six things that love does not do? What five things does love always do? Why does verse 13 say that love is the greatest?

2. Read Ephesians 5:22-30, preferably with your spouse. Together come up with a diagram of the way you feel the wife's submission and the husband's headship and sacrificial love should work in

real life situations. Wives are to submit to their husbands as to whom? Husbands are to love their wives as their own what?

3. Read 1 Corinthians 7:1-5. Why does the phrase, "It's my body!" not have a place in the marriage bed?

4. Genesis 2:18 records the first negative statement after a chapter full of "it was very good". In what ways do spouses help complete each other? Contrast this Scripture with 1 Corinthians 7:1 & 8. Are these statements contradictory?

5. First Corinthians 7:9 flatly says that if "they [the unmarried and the widows] cannot control themselves, they should marry, for it is better to marry than to burn with passion." Does this mean that physical fulfillment and sexual release are to be the primary purpose of marriage?

   *Note: Read in context; in many other Scriptures, Paul speaks highly of the married state (Ephesians 5:22-23;Colossians 3:18-19;1 Timothy 3:2,12; 5:14).

6. Proverbs 18:22 says, "He who finds a wife finds what is good." In its fullest sense, what does this verse mean? How are you "good" for your husband? In what ways could you improve?

 **Bits of Chocolate for Personal Reflection**

1. Of all love's attributes listed in 1 Corinthians 13, which is the hardest for you to practice? Why? Pray that God will help develop that trait in you.

2. Read 1 Corinthians 7 again, concentrating on verses 3-5. Are there times when you withhold lovemaking from your husband, either to punish or to manipulate things your way? If this is ever true, ask God to renew your desire to fulfill your husband sexually. It is always a good idea to ask Him to increase your physical desire for your husband. When your sex life is going great, don't forget to thank Him for this incredible expression of love.

A recent study on marital status and happiness found that married couples are 3.4 times more likely to be happy than cohabiting couples.

–Family Research Council, 2001

Puppy Chow

A favorite to make with the children.

Melt 1/2 cup peanut butter, 1 stick real butter &
1 12 oz. pkg. of milk chocolate chips over low heat,
stirring frequently until smooth.

Meanwhile put a medium box of Crispix cereal
and 1 cup oat cereal rings into a big bowl.

When chocolate mixture is melted,
pour over cereals and mix thoroughly.

Add 1 cup powdered sugar and coat thoroughly.
(You may put mixture into large baggies,
seal and let the children help shake
them up in order to coat
with powdered sugar)

Serve with big glasses
of milk & enjoy!

Chapter 5
Oh, Baby! (Ruth)

"A mother who is really a mother is never free."
–Honore de Balzac

I stared again at the double pink lines in disbelief. Even though I already knew I held in my hand a $5.94 stick, which confirmed my pregnancy, I grabbed the box and re-read the directions. *Any second line in the test window, no matter how faint, indicates a positive result. Consult your doctor, blah, blah, blah* . . . I shook the stick and banged it on the side of the sink wondering if that would change the results. I looked again. Nope. Still two brilliant, stubborn pink lines.

It had all started that morning when I wheeled the van into Wal-Mart and purchased a package of envelopes, a bottle of orange juice, a pregnancy test and two chocolate donuts. The cashier looked at me strangely, but, so what? I saved the receipt.

No wait, it actually started four weeks ago when we had that garage sale and sold the infant car seat, the stroller, the rattles, the baby clothes, and maternity clothes. *This baby will be a naked, bored safety hazard, I thought.*

Well, to be truthful, it must have begun six weeks ago on a gorgeous spring evening. The moon and stars twinkled like expensive diamonds on the black velvet backdrop at Zales. On sidewalk sale day. My husband and I sat on the porch swing sharing Cokes and a bag of peanuts in the shell. Our three children were peacefully asleep, upstairs in their rooms. We chatted, held hands and smooched and before you know it. . . . Well, that's not really suitable material for a book of this nature, but suffice to say that the Genesis One Rule kicked in. It's the rule that states that in view of the "be fruit-ful and multiply" command, hormones go into overdrive causing you to momentarily suspend belief in the seriousness of the procreative process. *It will never happen this once.*

And you could be so wrong. I have new respect for porch swings.

Thoughts hurtled through my head like so many Tinker Toy sculptures built on a rainy day. *Pregnancy tests are sold in the same aisle as, well in fact next to, prophylactics designed to prevent this very thing! Amazing.*

I had just finished teaching a set of abstinence classes for our local crisis pregnancy center. *I lectured all those students at the public high school about the fact that it only takes once. Now here I am in need of the center's services.*

How was I going to tell my husband about this surprise, fourth pregnancy? We had three little girls and had decided that our family was complete. In fact, we were just months away from his scheduled appointment at the doctor's office. The kind that specializes in helping those who have already fulfilled the whole fruitful command to stop it.

I am thirty-four years old. Isn't that too old to be having another baby? We'd have to put up with the snickers of our friends and the under-the-breath comments. *Don't you guys know what causes this yet?* Ha. Ha. Ha.

And then the meltdown. *I am going to have three children under the age of five! AUUAGGHHHH!!!!!*

I breathed deeply and prayed. I phoned my husband at work and asked him to take a little ride with me. Though he was mystified, he agreed. We chatted amiably about my writing deadlines and editing projects and the bad guys he needed to arrest and what trials were forthcoming. I racked my brain for a creative, cute way to tell him the news, just like I'd done with the other girls.

Sitting at the stoplight at 20th and St. Louis I figured it out. I burst out crying and threw the positive stick in his lap. Ever seen *Father of the Bride Part II?* If you have, picture the doctor's office scene. If you haven't, rent it tonight.

"HOW DID THIS HAPPEN?!" my husband demanded.

I lamely tried to explain my apparently fuzzy knowledge of the reproductive process. He glared.

"I *know* that. What I meant is, there haven't really been any, I mean the only time I can think of that we haven't taken, um, precautions, was. . . ." His voice trailed off, then he spluttered, "That particular night was one moment of temporary insanity!"

"Didn't you ever see that movie where Steve Martin and Diane Keaton find out that they're expecting after just one night on the kitchen floor? Our kitchen floor just happened to be a porch. Well, that, in a manner of speaking is what happened to us." I sat back, temporarily satisfied that I had explained everything. Not so.

"But that," he argued, "was a *movie!* Things like this just do *not* happen in my life!"

My poor only-child husband. I turned into the parking lot of the

Crisis Pregnancy Center and dropped him off. For about two minutes. Then I took pity on him and helped his bewildered self back into the passenger side.

In order to bolster our flagging self-confidence, I rattled off a list of all the "Things I Can Do/Things I Know" that qualified me for this adventure known as motherhood.

- I know how to clean up almost anything with spit.
- I know the fastest route to the bathroom of any Wal-Mart, Taco Bell or McDonald's in the United States.
- I know how to tell time using Sesame Street programs and Veggie Tales videos, as in "We'll be there in one Sesame Street and half a Veggie Tale."
- I have sung the Veggie Tales theme song in the middle of the produce aisle and have publicly sported stickers "awarded" me by my toddler and pre-schooler on various parts of my anatomy including, but not limited to, my shoulder, ear lobes, backside and left breast.
- I can drink a Coke with toddler floaties in it without experiencing nausea.
- I can finish the crusts of their leftover cheeseburgers and a few fries dropped on the van floor and call it a meal.
- I can boil water, unload the dishwasher, fold the clothes, talk on the phone and hand out after-school snacks with the baby on one hip.
- I can be intimate with my husband with one ear open for the baby crying and one eye on the door knob, making sure no toddler is trying to pick the lock.

I was vastly encouraged. Maybe we could do this again after all. I looked at him expectantly (no pun intended) after my recitation. No response.

"This will be our first *winter* baby. You know, none of my summer maternity clothes would have worked for this one anyway." Still silence.

I tried cheering him up. "Hey. Now we'll have an even number of children for amusement park rides and stuff."

This roused him. "I told you all three of them could bring friends and we'd still have an *even* number."

Apparently this was going to be harder than I thought. I tried a different tack. "Honey, this is quite a shock to me too, you know. But this week it already has a heart and a spine and even though it looks like a shrimp right now, it's *our* shrimp." I placed a hand protectively over my stomach. Shock wrestled with a dreamy tenderness. Wondrous excitement was rapidly winning out over trepidation. "We'll love this one just as much, you know."

"No question, we'll *love* it. How'll we *feed* it? Who's getting another job? The two-year-old, the four-year-old or the nine-year-old?"

Hormones kicked in again and I snuffled, wiping my nose back and forth across his dress shirt and leaving mascara traces everywhere along his collar like so many false eyelash pieces.

"Honey! I'm only kidding. Everything will be fine. Just give me a while to adjust."

"How long?" I demanded.

"Oh, about nine months." He bent down and rummaged for the miniature phone book we carry in the car.

"What are you doing?"

"I'm calling the Hawthorne Center to find out their visiting hours so you and the children can visit me while I'm in the little room with rubber walls!"

At that point I slugged him and he once again rose to the occasion and charmed me with that boyish grin. Furthermore, he promised to fetch me Milky Ways and Snicker Bars any time I craved them. My insides melted like, well, like chocolate. What a privilege to embark once again on such an adventure.

My sister and I have been beaten on the side of every major interstate in the Midwest. It had something to do with our propensity for acting like small beasts on vacation. As my weary mother said during one trip to Denver, Colorado, from our home in St. Louis, Missouri: "Colorado is beautiful; you just have to go through a lot of Kansas before you get there!" Didn't matter if we were actually traveling through Kansas on any given trip; my sister and I just made car excursions unbearable.

Despite the fact that my dad was of the "Every minute's a mile" school of travel and tossed us into the back seat at dawn, still pajama-clad, hoping against hope that we'd sleep most of the trip, we started in as he backed out of the drive. "I'm thirsty." "She touched me." "I have to go to the bathroom." "When are we gonna get there?"

The driveway was only eight feet long.

On one trip, my mother brought along a roll of masking tape [as a mother myself, I now know that she thought it suitable for several uses: binding our feet so we couldn't kick each other, taping our mouths shut, flinging it as a projectile] and used the tape to mark a line down the center of the back seat.

Finishing, she crawled back in the front seat with premature satisfaction. "There," she said, smiling and dusting her hands together, "Angie, you stay on your side; Cindy you stay on yours."

Approximately 2.5 miles into the trip my sister did the unthinkable. Scooting as close as possible to me without actually violating the taped boundary, she leaned her head into my space and gulped a huge breath of air. Under her breath she whispered, "I'm breathing your air!" Her accompanying grin smacked of evil. I promptly whacked her on top of the head with my latest Nancy Drew.

She wailed. I sat smugly. My mother sighed. My dad stopped the car. When he finished administering our annual vacation beating, my sister and I snuggled together, sitting precisely dead center of the taped line. We whispered about the meanness of our parents and plotted how we could run away at the next stop.

This saga is going to repeat itself with our children, I can already tell. Four of them and only two of us. No way are we going to have enough windows, drink holders, or unbroken crayons to last through any trip. And my husband and I are not alone in the secret desire to stop at a roadside park, leave them and drive away. . . . At least for three seconds.

We know this because some friends of ours recently told us that enroute to Georgia, they contemplated deserting their whining two-year-old at a truck stop in Birmingham, Alabama. But they saw several other toddlers there, too, wrecking the place.

Yep. I knew all about the ages and stages of motherhood.

Stage 1 - THE GLOW

During your first pregnancy, you begin wearing maternity clothes as soon as the lines turn pink. During your second pregnancy, remembering how frustrating it was to be limited to four outfits during your last trimester, and wearing, just for fun, your Monday outfit on a

Thursday, you try to wear your regular clothes as long as possible. By your third pregnancy, your maternity clothes ARE your regular clothes!

I don't even want to think about the fourth. I told my husband that his only job was to weigh more than me no matter what.

The first time around, you refuse to be horrified by the labor stories of other women, figuring it couldn't be that bad or so many people wouldn't be having babies. Besides, those little breathing classes you go to with your husband are soooo cute! Once in labor, however, the only breathing you're doing is spouting threats about cutting off his breath! In all subsequent pregnancies, you acknowledge that labor is a cruel euphemism for lots of pain and you ask for an epidural in your eighth month.

When Eden, our oldest, was an infant, I boiled every pacifier and toy she dropped. With Emily, I rinsed things off in the sink. When Elizabeth arrived, I wiped things off on my jeans. If she had already popped it, dirt and all into her mouth, I just sighed and asked her if it was good.

A friend of mine mailed me this behavior pattern from the Internet. With the first baby you spend a good bit of every day just gazing at the baby. With the second child, you spend a bit of every day watching to be sure that your older child isn't squeezing, poking or hitting the baby. [This is so true. When Baby Ellie was a few weeks old and my middle daughter, Emmy, was barely two, I sat on the couch nursing with Emmy snuggled up next to me. Suddenly Emmy opened her mouth wide ala JAWS, just behind the baby's tiny head and announced, "Mommy, I REALLY need to bite the baby Ellie!"] When the third baby arrives, you spend a little bit of every day hiding from the children.

Still, this short, sweet infancy stage has many delicious chocolate moments to savor. The hour spent nursing or rocking your baby just before dawn. Listening to the squirmy puppy noises of your newborn. Bending your head over his soft downy one, inhaling that "new baby" smell.

Stage 2 - THE GRINCH

All too soon the infant stage is history and they grow like weeds slathered with Miracle Gro. I think it's significant that Mother's Day is celebrated during the same month that is designated as "Mental Health Month"; don't you? As our children grow older, we mothers have to make increasingly unpopular decisions. At times our sanity teeters. Our best efforts are sometimes met with eye rolling, foot stomping and door slamming. Yet the role of Grinch is a difficult, but necessary one to play.

The battle of wills begins early. When our oldest daughter, Eden, was three, a nightly bedtime battle took place. She went to bed wonderfully; she just wouldn't stay there. The fourth time she ventured out after various requests for drinks, bathroom breaks and "just one more story," I got firm. "Eden, if you don't get back in that bed and stay there, Mommy is going to give you swats!"

She contemplated this for a moment and then questioned, "How many?" I had to leave the room in order to have a private laugh behind the refrigerator.

We must discipline our children. No one else wields our influence. Kay Cole James, Secretary of Health during the Reagan-Bush administration, is a lovely, classy, African-American woman. At one conference, she had this to say about discipline. "I see women today who seem afraid to discipline their children. They have been brought up in an age where reasoning, distraction and elaborate psychology rule the discipline books. I wholeheartedly disagree. We need to take back our children! When our children were small, our family attended a Southern church that was integrated . . . because we went there! It wasn't real hard to figure out whose children were doing the misbehaving. So my husband and I determined that we would not be embarrassed by our children."

During the dark chocolate days we just have to remember the eleventh commandment: Thou shalt not assume thy children shall thank thee until they're grown and have children of their own!

Impending parenthood changes us intrinsically from the moment we find out we're pregnant. Hearts, lives, and furniture are rearranged to accommodate new life. Our lives, our time, indeed, our very bodies will never be the same. We allow our wombs to be hotel rooms for nine months and we spend the next nine months trying to stuff stretch marks and flabby tummies back into our pre-baby jeans. Simple excursions to the grocery store need mountains of equipment. Strollers. Diaper bag with diapers, wipes, ointment, pacifiers, rattles, and blankets. Car seats. Infant carriers. Sippy cups. Snack boxes. At times we feel more like combination nursing cats and pack mules than women.

When we become parents, we break all the rules we had in our BC (before children) days about what our children would and wouldn't do. We break the vow not to tell cute kid stories to anyone who will listen (did I tell you about the time that Eden. . . .) and despite our best efforts, we end up dragging out a wallet full of pictures whenever anyone asks.

Although there are days when we *long* for an escape, we find that when we get away from the children, we spend a large part of the time missing them, thinking about them, buying them souvenirs and noticing all the things they'd enjoy if they were with us. In short, nothing is too good for our children and nobody can ever do enough for them.

It's like the story of the mother of a young boy. They were staying at a fashionable resort and every day the boy went swimming in the lake. Couldn't wait to dive into the water! One day he swam out too far. The mother, watching him, screamed for the lifeguard.

The lifeguard dove and went under several times before locating the boy. He swam to shore and laid the boy's lifeless body on the beach, performing CPR seemingly in vain. The mother begged him not to give up, and finally the boy stirred, spat up some water and opened his eyes. His mother grabbed the boy to her chest and turned to the lifeguard. Rather than saying, "Thank you for saving his life," as you might expect, she said, "He also had a hat!"

Stage 3 - THE GAIN

It's been said that children are the world's greatest suspense story – you have to wait an entire generation before knowing how they turn out!

I always had a great relationship with my parents, but I have to admit that during high school, I sometimes thought they were the dumbest people on earth. When I went away to college I found that they must have been taking classes too, because man, they got smarter!

Undoubtedly there will be tough times before the reward. There will be prodigal moments when we wait for our children to return to values and to home. There will be nights that are too short and days that are too long. Raising children is a lifelong commitment that requires sacrifice and tenacious love. Exactly like that God has for us. What a wonder that we are called both His children and His friends.

Hang in there, mothers. At the end of the journey, you'll find that you've made a friend.

On my dresser sits a bundle of small sticks tied with pink satin and white eyelet ribbon. Emmy collected them for me when she was three. "I thought you would want these so you'll remember how much I love you today. And foyever!" she added exuberantly. She threw chubby arms around my knees and I forgave her for every past and future transgression.

Recently, on a family trip [did I mention the drive was 22 hours?] to Scottsdale, Arizona, my husband began frantically looking at our atlas. I peered over his shoulder to offer my assistance. It was then that I heard him muttering: "Where is that truck stop in Birmingham?"

And what of our fourth most precious surprise? My husband and I practically flew on wings into the doctor's office for our twelve-week check-up. This day was hear-the-baby's-heartbeat day. My husband expectantly pulled up a chair and held my hand, grinning. The nurse applied cold, wet goo to the slight bulge on my stomach.

"Hmmm, that baby must be hiding. They're only about 2 1/4 inches long at this stage. Why don't you step across to the ultrasound room?"

We did. This would be even better. A first picture of this miraculous surprise. The technician wielded the instrument like a magic wand. I strained my eyes for a glimpse. There was a hole in the sac and a leak in my heart.

They took us back across the hall to the examining room. After a few centuries of seconds, the doctor walked in. My hands twisted with Greg's like a wet mop wringing out dirty water. I held my breath.

"Greg, Cindy, I'm sorry. Your baby must have died sometime in the last two weeks. We can't tell exactly when and there's no way to tell why. I am so very sorry."

Dark chocolate boiled over me in hot scalding ways. Sharp pains and sentence prayers formed like phantoms. *God, thank you for my three beautiful, healthy children at home.*

I gulped down huge drinks of sorrow. God, I want to believe you know best. Please help me. My heart is broken. I never knew I could love two inches of anything so much.

It won't always be easy, but then things worth doing rarely are. These years will be over before you know it, so don't blink. You won't want to miss a second.

And those Birmingham moments? Well, they'll always be there, but don't dwell in that town too long. Most of the time you have the world by the tail and you don't even know it.

". . . and a little child shall lead them."

–Isaiah 11:6

POSTSCRIPT:

After the loss of our surprise fourth pregnancy, I wasn't sure I wanted to end my childbearing years on such a sad note. After much discussion and prayer, my husband and I decided to try for eight weeks. If God thought we should add to our blessings, we would be delighted; if not, we would be contented.

Elexa Rose Dagnan was born eleven months later.
She will turn two years old in the summer of 2003.
Her mother is thirty-six and surviving. God is faithful!

 ## Gaining a Chocolate Perspective

1. Read Isaiah 7:14;11:6 and 19:6. What is so wonderful about the fact that Jesus came to earth as a baby, helpless and small, rather than as a grown man?

2. Luke 1:80 says of Jesus' cousin, John the Baptist, "And the child grew and became strong in spirit." What do you think the phrase "strong in spirit" means?

3. Compare that statement about John with the one about Jesus in Luke 2:52. "And Jesus grew in wisdom and stature, and in favor with God and men." How might their upbringings have been similar? Different?

4. Joel 1:3, Exodus 10:2, and Deuteronomy 6:7-9 speak of telling our children and our children's children about the things of the Lord. His commandments. His wrath against the Egyptians. His deliverance of his people. We get to take that a step further, for we have the privilege of being able to share the fulfillment of the Messiah's birth, rather than just the promise. How are you working the things of God into your daily life and the lives of the people, especially the children, with whom you come in contact?

**Bits of Chocolate for
Personal Reflection**

1. What is the most challenging part of parenting for you? Why? If you do not have children, what do you suspect would be the most challenging part of parenting? Why?

2. What situations are most likely to become "Birmingham Moments" with your children? How do you cope?

3. Imagine yourself as Jesus' mother. Read the entire second chapter of Luke. From Christ's birth through his visit to teach in the temple at age twelve, what observations can you make about Jesus' character and religious education?

4. Psalm 127:3 states that sons [children] are a heritage from the Lord. In this context, heritage can almost be defined as a privilege. Spend some time with your children today, and as you do so, thank God that He has loaned these precious gifts to you.

The Fake
Neiman Marcus Story
Cookie Recipe

Even though the story isn't true,
the cookies are truly delicious!

Neiman's (alleged) $250 Cookie Recipe

1 cup butter

1 cup sugar

1 cup brown sugar

2 eggs

1 teaspoon vanilla

2 cups flour

2 1/2 cups oatmeal

1/2 teaspoon salt

1 teaspoon baking powder

1 teaspoon baking soda

12 oz. chocolate chips

1/2 8 oz. grated Hershey Bar

1/2 cup chopped nuts (optional)
(in my humble opinion,
nuts ruin cookies)

Cream butter w/ both sugars. Add eggs and vanilla. Mix together w/ flour, oatmeal, salt, baking powder and baking soda. Add chips, candy and nuts. Roll into balls, about the size of walnuts and place two inches apart on cookie sheet. Bake for 6-7 minutes at 350 degrees. Makes lots of yummy cookies.

Chapter 6

Three Musketeers

"It's the friends you can call at 4 a.m. that matter."
—Marlene Dietrich

The early spring rains had been exceptionally heavy. A thoroughly disgusted farmer sat next to his stalled tractor that was in mud up to its axles. His neighbor came over and said, "Tell you what Jim. I'll give it a try with my tractor."

" 'Ppreciate it, neighbor. But what if you just get stuck too?"

"Then I'll come and sit in the mud with you." Now that's a friend!

Debbie is one such friend. The story of our friendship began long before we ever met. When I was in high school, my daddy and I prayed every night for me to find a truly special friend. One with whom I would share not only common interests, but also a strong faith in the Lord. One who would be loyal, trustworthy, and adventurous. In short, my absolutely favorite compliment—stunning!

During high school, I had many friends. I was indescribably close to most of my youth group (How could I forget going to Steak 'n' Shake for cheesecake and fries or having sand poured in my hair while I was asleep on a camp out & float trip! You know who you are!). I had many school friends as well. But each time I thought I had found what Anne Shirley so aptly called a "bosom friend," something happened.

I finally arrived at college, just four days after my eighteenth birthday. It was my first ever move away from home and I was as green as they come. I was eager to set things up in my new dorm room, alternately wanting and dreading to meet the new roommate. I finally did. What a mutual dislike at first glance! She had already been there for over a year and strolled in with confidence, looking disdainfully at my colorful sundress and matching sandals. She looked up at the ceiling with great interest.

"Hi! I'm Cindy! I have to sing at chapel on Thursday, and the music director said you'd play for me!" I added shyly. "He says you're awesome!"

Her jaw set. "Oh, he did?" She glanced around the room at my voluminous baggage, boxes, books, and stacks (let's just say I'm not a one-bag kind of gal). "All this is yours?" This in an incredulous tone.

I fluffed my brand-new comforter across my bunk. "Garfield?! I despise Garfield!" she muttered under her breath.

I looked across at her side of the room, already neatly made up; her comforter had a beautiful brown and rose sprigged bedspread. I could kind of see what she meant.

Now to be fair to Debbie, I'll give you a short background. I arrived on campus a few days later than most of the students; I had just flown in from a national pageant in Florida. Our dorm mom (who strangely enough retired after I graduated) had pulled Debbie aside and informed her that she was getting a "special" roommate. I would need some extra attention, she warned Debbie. And everything Debbie saw that day confirmed it.

Still wearing expensive clothes from a wonderful wardrobe that had been donated to me for the pageant from several exclusive St. Louis boutiques (what she didn't know was that after years of wearing lots of hand-me-downs growing up as preacher's daughter, this was a new and heady experience for me) and sobbing because my parents had just left, I must have made quite the impact.

To shorten a long and wonderful story, let's just say that we agreed to go to the Dean of Students and request a change of roommates. We went to his office and told him that we just wouldn't be able to get along. "Girls," he steepled his fingers against his chin, "according to the personality profile that we give all of our incoming students, you two are a perfect match. I want you to stick it out for the rest of the semester. If I'm wrong about this, I'll move you."

Not only did we not move, but we roomed together for the next three years! She ended up being my permanent accompanist for chapel, voice lessons, concerts, and competitions. She once typed one of my papers at *three* a.m. as I dictated it to her. I was busy typing a second one; both were due at seven a.m. the next morning. We broke curfew together. We survived five semesters on little more than Domino's Pizza, Funyons, M&Ms, and Diet Coke. We were in each other's weddings. Her daughter, Cara, and my oldest daughter were born one day apart. We exchange letters and holiday and birthday gifts. When we get together, it's as though time has never moved forward.

She has seen me at my absolute worst (both appearance and behavior wise) and loves me still (even during a brief "closet slob" stage when she put a masking tape line down the center of our room and told me to at least keep my junk on my own side!). We have been through a lot of hard things together. We have prayed for each other. We have shopped, giggled fitfully after too many sleepless nights and critiqued each other's college dates. We have cried together. We discovered that we both adore *Gone With the Wind* [she didn't crack a smile when I once told her it was my ambition to marry a Christian Rhett Butler!] and *Anne of Green Gables*. We were both PKs. We both think that Big Macs are the only things worth ordering at McDonald's. That we'd rather read than do just about anything else with our free time. We have encouraged dreams. We have traded and kept confidences.

She's a "David & Jonathan" kind of friend. That's why I wasn't surprised when she drove nine hours from her home in Texas to help me shop for a dress to wear to my daddy's funeral. She sat on my couch with my two-day-old infant and me and sobbed with me. She knew my heart was broken. She drove another five hours to the funeral in St. Louis, just so I'd know she was there. She's that kind of friend.

Thinking about friendship and chocolate in the same chapter naturally made me think about a recipe for friendship. It seems that though there are several types of friendships, there are several common ingredients that they all need.

A RECIPE FOR FRIENDSHIP

3 cups of acceptance

1 cup of maintenance

2 cups each of respect & encouragement

4 slices of fun

1 heaping tablespoon of adventure

1 level teaspoon of accountability

Add a liberal sprinkle of laughter

Brush with commitment glaze

Bake for as long as needed under the
sunshine of God's abundant mercy

First of all, friendship requires acceptance. You must acknowledge a friend's weaknesses, but look past them and help encourage her strengths and potential.

I was the only one in my home economics class given extra credit for NOT wearing the garment I made to class. In my ambitious desire to make the dreaded class worthwhile, I opted for a complex Laura Ashley pattern, a skirt and blouse with three coordinating fabrics. Aside from the fact that it took sixteen "ripping out" sessions [all conducted under the watchful eyes of my teacher, who all the while took deep huffy breaths, as Junie B. would say, slumping her shoulders in disgust], there was that little matter about the two inch chunks missing from one side of the garment before we figured out that since I was left-handed, specially made scissors might be best. On the finished blouse (and I use that term loosely) one sleeve cut off my circulation while the other flapped violently as though it were preparing for take-off.

It only becomes a source of contention at Halloween. In my opinion this is just one more reason that the wretched holiday is not a Christian one. The children of my seamstress friends show up in adorable hand-sewn costumes. [I still haven't gotten over the lion!] However, if my mother isn't available to make my poor girls' costumes, they are the ones who show up wearing an assortment of cardboard boxes, tattered pajamas, and droopy balloons, poorly attached to their "costume" with hot glue and duct tape. It is one of my friends' running jokes to ask me if I've made my outfit and then lose their collective breath laughing. Ha.

My cooking skills aren't much better, but that's another story for another day. My girlfriends love me anyway.

However, friendships cannot stay green without some maintenance and watering. A wise proverb says, "On the road between the houses of friends grass does not grow." A wise friend does not neglect a relationship. Send a card for no reason at all. Keep up with her life. Remember birthday and anniversary dates. Mail her a prayer you've prayed for her during a difficult time. Plan a quarterly date for dinner out. Go see a movie with a huge pack of friends. Host a cookie exchange. Meet at Wal-Mart after the kids go to bed for grocery shopping and bonding!

Friendship cannot be all about need either, or it becomes drudgery. Fun must be included. How grateful I am to my book club pals for this friendship ingredient. Vickie, Sharris, Lindsey, Patty, Karen, and Lori are pure fun. They are witty, intelligent, and affirming. Our monthly meetings to expand both our horizons and our waistlines are an oasis of comfort, despite the fact that I have ended up lost on the way to every single one of their homes.

Friendship also provides a strong catalyst for adventure. Contrary to popular belief, adventure is not the same thing as fun. They are not mutually exclusive, but neither are they interchangeable. Though I could share many stories with you about adventures in friendship, my trip with Julie remains unsurpassed. For fourteen whirlwind days, Julie and I toured Europe, including the place I had longed to go all my life. Paris. Beginning my sophomore year of high school, I dreamed about visiting. Paris. The city of lights. The city of romance. The Tour Eiffel. The Arc D'Triomphe. Sigh.

Specifically, I wanted to be kissed underneath the Arc D'Triomphe. On our last evening in Paris, we dined at a charming outdoor cafe. It was Julie's birthday. It was also the last opportunity, probably in my whole life, I thought, to fulfill my lifelong dream.

Right after dinner, I started in on her. "Jewels. I want you to help me scout out someone suitable for kissing. He needs to be kind of cute at least, but also non-threatening. Okay? Okay?"

Julie rolled her eyes. "You can't be serious! You are not really going through with this!"

"But Jewels, I absolutely have to! I mean, what if I never, ever get the chance again?!"

Before long, we spotted a group of American soldiers standing near the Arc. Julie pointed out two of them to me. After a quick reconnaissance trip, I chose my man. I walked up to him, Julie trailing behind with the camera, ready to snap a shot for my Europe adventure scrapbook.

I cleared my throat and tapped him on the shoulder. He turned to me and smiled. I still cannot believe that I had the courage and stupidity to pull this off. "Uh, I was wondering if you could do me a favor . . . my friend Julie" – I motioned frantically for her to stand by me for moral support – "and I are visiting here, but for a really long time, I have thought that it would be so wonderful to be kissed underneath the Arc D'Triomphe, but I . . . well, I need somebody to kiss me!"

His friend elbowed him sharply in the rib cage. "Sure!" he replied kindly. "Do you want to lead, or should I?"

"Ummm," I stammered, "Well, it's been a while for me, so maybe you should. Oh, and one other thing. Could my friend take just one picture so I can prove that it actually happened?"

It was dusk. We positioned ourselves under the Arc so Julie could get a picture of the evening, of the French tri-color flag, and the two of us – kissing.

He kissed me. My face turned scarlet. I broke away and stammered. "Thank you." Then I fled across the traffic that circled the Arc, completely forgetting about the understreet pathway. Nearly got myself killed. Oh well, it was an adventure. Julie caught up with me and repeated fifteen times in a row, "I can't believe you did that. I cannot believe you did that!" And then she squealed, "You did it!"

The travel reporter for the *Los Angeles Times* happened to be on our tour. He reported my adventure in the next week's newspaper. Turns out that a woman who lived in Joplin, Missouri, got a copy of their travel pages mailed to her by her sister from California every week. One evening, I got a phone call at my house.

"Hello? Is this Cindy? The Cindy who was featured in the *Los Angeles Times* travel article on Europe?"

"Yes, it is." I was confused. "May I help you?"

"Well, I read that article and I just have to know – did you really kiss that soldier underneath the Arc D'Triomphe?"

"Yes, ma'am. I sure did." I told her all about the background of my lifelong dream. "So," I concluded, "I just decided to go for it!"

"Good for you! I'm eighty years old and I just wanted to tell you how glad I am that you aren't letting the adventures in life pass you by. It was nice talking to you. Good-bye!"

I hung up with a light heart, feeling a kinship with this stranger-friend.

A few days later I got my pictures back. I framed the one of the Paris kiss as a reminder that dreams do come true. It remained there until my wedding day.

"The best way to mend a broken heart is time and girlfriends."
—Gwyneth Paltrow

True friends are also "balcony people." They are champion encouragers. My mother is one such lady. Whenever I have looked out at an audience from any stage I have ever been on in my life, she has been there, waving like crazy.

I have many friends who will have proofread chapters or parts of chapters or listened to so many ideas that they will be sick of them. But they will still come to my book signings and pretend to be total strangers, admiring my work.

Scripture says, "The kisses of an enemy may be profuse, but faithful are the wounds of a friend" (Proverbs 27:6). True friends are willing to share the truth with you, even when it's not easy. They are willing to hold you accountable, to put your feet to the fire when necessary.

A beautiful new song by Watermark *(More Than You Know)* expresses this thought with simple eloquence: "You have spoken the truth over my life." Ah, the joy of having such a friend.

Writer George Elliot once penned, "It is never too late to be what you might have become." Real friends know the truth of this and don't stop prodding you until you agree to begin the hard process of becoming.

Find a trustworthy friend to whom you can be accountable. Share your struggles and temptations with that friend. Cultivate transparency. Pray for each other. Get comfortable enough and tough enough that you can take brutal honesty, if necessary, packaged with the wrapping of unconditional love.

Even as I finish this chapter, my friend Tammy is sitting at my kitchen table, proofing chapters, red pen in hand, ready to speak the truth (in love, I hope). That in itself might not be such a sacrifice, but it's ten o'clock at night and she drove over just because I asked. (Okay, begged.) All this I got for the price of a warm hug and a cold Vanilla Coke.

"People are lonely because they build walls instead of bridges," wrote Joseph Fort Newton. Try reaching out and scaling those walls with the bridge of friendship. Be the first to greet someone new at work or at church. Extend an invitation to do something simple on neutral ground. [I picked up a new walking buddy and a new friend just because another friend and I rescued her from a semi-permanent, post-partum position on her couch.] Sometimes we lack friends only because we miss the opportunities to make them.

Perhaps the recipe for committed friendship is best described in the story of Jonathan and David (1 Samuel 18-20). Jonathan became a close friend to David. Close enough that Scripture records that Jonathan "became one in spirit with David, and he loved him as himself" (18:1). There was just one big glitch: Jonathan's father, King Saul, hated David's guts and wanted to kill him. Whenever the King heard David's name, he threw a royal fit. On more than one occasion Jonathan saved David's life.

In Chapter 20, however, David realizes that the threat is worsening. He entreats Jonathan to warn him so he can flee to safety. Don't miss the significance of Jonathan's reply: "Whatever you want me to do, I'll do for you" (20:4). Jonathan and David make a pact. Jonathan prays for the Lord to call David's enemies to account. In return, David promises not to cut off his kindness to Jonathan's family, even when he becomes the next king of Israel.

For the next several chapters Saul and David chase each other around the hills, Saul trying desperately to take David's life. Several times David has the chance to kill Saul, but he spares him. Eventually both Saul and Jonathan are killed in the heat of battle. David mourns, but he does not forget his promise.

In 2 Samuel 9:1 David specifically looks for a way to keep his word. "Is there anyone still left of the house of Saul to whom I can show kindness for Jonathan's sake?" He took Mephibosheth, Jonathan's crippled son under his wing and provided for him and " he always ate at the king's table. . . ."

Friends sweeten all of life with their comforting, chocolate presence. How much richer our existence when they are near. Friends we can vent to, cry with, giggle with, shop with, engage in girl-talk with, dissect men's psyches with and debate the best panty hose and deodorant brands with—what unparalleled luxury! We love stories with strong girlfriend themes: *Thelma & Louise, Steel Magnolias, Divine Secrets of the Ya-Ya Sisterhood, the Sweet Potato Queens*, and Vickie Iovine's *Girlfriend's Guide to . . .* series. They appeal to the wonderful club of which we are members, just by virtue of birth: the universal club of girlfriendness!

> *Oh, the comfort, the inexpressible comfort of*
> *feeling safe with a person;*
> *having neither to weigh thoughts nor measure words, but to*
> *pour them all out, just as they are, chaff and grain together,*
> *knowing that a faithful hand will take and sift them,*
> *keep what is worth keeping, and then,*
> *with the breath of kindness,*
> *blow the rest away.*
>
> –George Eliot

Of course all of this is but a shadow of the greatest friend; the one who sticks closer than a brother. The one who died because He loved you more than life itself. "What a friend we have in Jesus. . . ."

Just today I sat around a small round table in a room at the back of our church. A group of us were there to pray, study God's Word and apply it to our lives. We bared our souls. One precious friend shared a poignant and personal breakthrough. She smiled through her tears, obviously needing a Kleenex.

"That story," I said, "is definitely worth using one of my fancy yellow ladybug print tissues for! My sister sent them all the way from Taiwan with this note attached, 'I thought these were so cute! But you don't spend this much money on Kleenex and use them on your own nose!'"

We laughed and cried. A microcosm of friendship at a round table, bathed in the ever-present sunshine of His inestimable love.

"In the cookies of life,
friends are the chocolate chips."

–Seen on a coffee mug

 **Gaining a**
Chocolate Perspective

1. Take a block of time and read, really read, 1 Samuel 18-20. List three friendship qualities that you find at the heart of Jonathan's and David's story.

2. Proverbs 27:6 says, ". . . faithful are the wounds of a friend." Has there ever been a time when you have been called upon to be a "faithful wounder?" Did you do your job, or did you opt to tell the friend what they wanted to hear?
What was the outcome?

3. Matthew 11:9 describes Jesus as a "friend of tax collectors and sinners." Do you know of anyone to whom you could extend a hand of friendship, but have been reluctant to do so?
What keeps you from seeking out people in need of friendship that might be outside your comfort zone?

4. The friendship recipe in this chapter calls for several ingredients:
   • acceptance
   • maintenance
   • respect & encouragement
   • fun & adventure
   • accountability
   • laughter
   • commitment

   Which of those ingredients are the easiest for you to bring to a friendship? Which are the hardest?
   Is there another ingredient you would like to add?

5. James 2:23 says Abraham was called God's friend. What do you think it takes to be a friend of God? Are the requirements vastly different than those of being a friend to anyone else? Why or why not?

Bits of Chocolate for Personal Reflection

1. Proverbs 17:17 says, "A friend loves at all times." First Samuel 18:1 says that Jonathan loved David as himself. Are you that kind of friend? Think over your list of friends and honestly evaluate what you "put into it." Plan to show some gesture of appreciation to at least one friend this week. If you have a friend that you've neglected, give them a call.

2. Someone once said, "Nothing is as hard to do gracefully as coming down off your high horse!" How gracefully do you take true and constructive criticism from your friends? How would you like someone to approach you with an issue or character trait he or she felt was a problem?

The First Chocolate Recipe Cindy Ever Learned to Make
During 7th grade Home Economics

Chocolate Layered Dessert

1ST LAYER:
- 2 1/2 cups flour
- 1/2 cup pecans, chopped
- 1 1/2 sticks butter, melted

Blend and press into a 9 X 13 pan. Bake at 325 degrees for 20 minutes. Cool and set aside.

2ND LAYER:
- 1 cup sugar
- 8 oz. cream cheese
- 1/2 of 13 1/2 oz. container of Cool Whip

3RD LAYER:
- 1 large pkg. chocolate pudding mix
- 1 small chocolate pudding mix

Mix pudding mixes with 3 cups of milk until thick and spread over 2nd layer. Refrigerate at least one hour. (This is very important. Trust me.)

4TH LAYER:
Spread remaining half of Cool Whip over top of 3rd layer. Sprinkle with nuts.

"Real friends are those who, when you feel you've made a fool of yourself, don't feel you've done a permanent job."

–Unknown

Chapter 7
Chocolate in the Pot
(So Many Pieces, So Little Time!)

"Nothing really belongs to us but time,
which even he has who has nothing else."

–Baltasar Gracian

What was my stunning beginning for this chapter? I forgot.

Ever gone to the refrigerator, opened the door and gazed into its sticky depths unable to remember what you wanted?

Ever slammed the car door in a hurry to be on time to yet another commitment only to see your locked-in keys dangling mockingly from the ignition?

Ever run upstairs for something and wandered around each room trying to remember that illusive item you sought?

It's not entirely an aging thing. It's short-term memory loss induced by a culture that is sleep-deprived and over-committed.

I live at a near frantic pace these days. The sad truth of it is that most of my schedule is my fault. Most of my friends are in the same boat. We have spent so much time pursuing our days that they have now revolted and are pursuing us! We are fleeing an enemy largely of our own making. Time. The one thing we never seem to have enough of.

As you know, one of my all time favorite films is *Gone With the Wind*. In one scene the camera pans a sundial at *Twelve Oaks*, a beautiful Southern plantation. It was engraved with this message: *"Do not squander time. It is the stuff life is made of."* Time has wings and it flies whether you're having fun or not. We know this, but in our endless pursuit of having things, doing things, learning things, and going places, we have become a nation of time-squanderers. Not a pretty thing to admit.

Think of all the things that have taken place in your day that you can never repeat or recreate in exactly the same way.

- A spontaneous hug from a chocolate-covered toddler, fresh from licking the beaters.
- Paying the bills and taking the time to bow your head with gratitude that there is money to mail them out.

- Watering the cherry red geraniums on the front porch.
- Finishing a novel that left you teary-eyed and wanting more.
- Pushing your baby or grandchild in a swing and hearing that delightful belly laugh.
- Meeting a new friend whom you know will become a kindred spirit.
- The children's delight at the grocery store sprinkler, washing the vegetables.
- An unexpected visit.

Ordinary things, but irreplaceable, just the same. We can never reclaim an exact moment, good or bad. Time is the one thing once spent, that we can never have back.

Yet it's almost as if we're afraid to stop doing and start being. Or better still, start becoming. We have become convinced that hurry is the same as productivity. Worse yet, though we're exhausted, we equate hurry with fulfillment. Pastor and author John Ortberg calls this "hurry sickness." You've got it if you're already skipping ahead to the next paragraph. You've got it if you push the elevator button five times even though it's already lit. You've got it if you mutter hatefully under your breath at traffic lights, "Come on, come on! I've got to get moving." You've got it if your last three suppers have been eaten from drive-thru windows. You've got it if you no longer care about quality relationships or leisure. You just want to get things done. Lots of them. Right now.

Ortberg recalls the time he called a wise spiritual mentor for some direction. His friend paused for a long while. "You must ruthlessly eliminate hurry from your life," he said slowly.

"Okay, I've written that one down, "Ortberg told him impatiently. "Now what else is there?"

We grin, but much of the time we're the same. We want a magic formula, a quick fix for our out-of-control schedules. We mentally skip ahead in our conversations. In our mind, our fingers are turning frenetic circles. *Okay, already. Get to the point. Can't you talk any faster?* Wonder if we'd ever have any friendships if people could read our minds?

We drive in the fast lane on the interstate. We talk on our cell phones at stoplights and in the checkout lanes at the grocery stores. We haul our laptops on plane trips and do too much of an insidious thing called multi-tasking.

Ortberg even suggests that "we worship at the shrine of the Golden

Arches not because they sell good food or even cheap food but *fast* food." But even after this marvelous invention, we were required to – gasp – get *out* of our cars and go into the restaurant to get the food and eat it. "So," Ortberg continues tongue-in-cheek, "we invented the drive-thru lane. Now families can eat in vans, as God intended."

Ouch. My own little girls are ridiculously over-joyed when we tell them we get to go out to eat. One of them, usually laid-back, sweet little Emmy, questions, "Do we even get to go inside, or do we have to eat in our boosters?" Their reaction on the too rare occasions when the answer is – "Inside!" – tells me a little too much about the pace of our lives.

The good news is, at least hurry sickness isn't terminal. There is a difference between being busy and being in a hurry. I know this, and yet if I had a dime for every time I say something to my girls along the lines of, "Hurry up, we're gonna be late!" "Okay, girls, let's head 'em up and move 'em out!" Or "What are you doing with all those Barbie shoes? We don't have time for that right now." I could probably guarantee the permanent existence of the Social Security system!

I've gotten in such a habit of hurry that sometimes I say it out of, well, out of habit. Thankfully, children can be so wise. Sometimes I badger Ellie about hurrying through her bath. She draws it out for hours. Loves bubbles. Wraps up the soap in washcloths. Takes care of her two rubber ducks. Pretends that the drain whispers secret messages. Wiggles. Splashes. Generally delights in water and nakedness. "Hurry up, Ellie!" My voice rings with impatience.

And with one question she draws me up short. "Why're you grumpy mommy? What'd I do now?"

I have to answer truthfully, humbly, and apologetically. "Nothing." Then together we do what in our house is known as "frolicking." My little girls and I (and sometimes, even Greg) join hands and dance in a little circle in celebration of some small occasion of pure joy. We need to do it more often.

My daddy used to tease that we're all terminal, some of us are just going sooner than others! And though we know this to be true, we rush through our days ignoring and overlooking the daily pleasures of the ordinary. Sometimes we need a gentle reminder to take some of the pieces out of the pot so life can be savored.

My Friend Melissa's Wonderful
Chocolate-Dipped Peanut Butter Cookies
Adapted from a dessert booklet by Borden

- 1 14 oz. can Eagle Brand sweetened condensed milk
- 1 cup peanut butter
  (Melissa's killer secret is to use honey nut flavored p.b.)
- 1 egg
- 1 teaspoon vanilla
- 2 cups biscuit mix

With mixer, blend all ingredients. Chill dough for one hour. Bake in 350 degree oven for 6-8 minutes. (Do not overbake.)

Meanwhile, melt 1 pound chocolate bark.

When cookies are baked and cooled, partially dip each cookie into the melted chocolate bark. Place on wax paper until set.

Chocolate Choices (Living Your Priorities)

Without sounding glib, the simple truth is we all make choices every day. Choices to live or just exist. To merely wonder about something, or to take action. To cook from scratch or to order take out. To heat the Pop Tart or eat it cold. We also make choices about what to do (or not to do) with our time. Twenty-four hours. 1,440 minutes. 866,400 seconds. Every day. In just one year we have 31,536,000 seconds. 525,600 minutes. 8,760 hours. 365 days.

This statement was on a flip calendar I once had. "Your datebook is your creed. What you believe in, you have time for." Do our schedules truly reflect our hearts, at least the way we want them to be? We need to remember that life is comprised of time, so we need to live life intentionally. Deliberately.

So how do we make wise choices with our time? One way is to analyze (truthfully) where our time goes. I suggest making two pie (let's make them chocolate pie) graphs. Write down a simple list of your main activities. Divide one pie into the appropriate number of pieces, drawing larger pieces for things you spend a lot of time on, making the pieces successively smaller, depending on the time spent. No cheating. Make the graph reflect a typical day.

Now get out a green (or any color, I'm practicing not being controlling) pen and circle the three items from the list that you would consider to be your top priorities. Shade those pieces of pie the same color. Now compare. Do they match?

Next, take some time and draw pieces of pie in the second graph so that they reflect your *ideal* day. As you draw, consider these questions: What legacy do I want to leave? What do I want to do most? What am I passionate about? Remember, too, that some time commitments refresh, rather than drain us. My book club and Bible study groups are two such items for me, so I make sure I can attend them both. When you finish, post your pie somewhere that you can easily refer to it when you plan your days and pray for your personal needs.

Goal-Setting

There is only so much of you to go around and only so much available time. I like Stephen Covey's statement: "The 'good' is the enemy of the 'best'." It's so difficult to say "No" to good things. Good causes. Good people. But it is *necessary*. Therefore, a second useful tool is goal-setting.

In the Rogers & Hammerstein musical *South Pacific*, Bloody Mary sings a cheery, fabulous phrase during a song called, "Happy Talk." *"You got to have a dream, if you don't have a dream, how you gonna make a dream come true?"*

Put your finger between these pages, put your head back and your feet up for a few moments. Let your mind drift. What did you want to be when you were ten years old? Sixteen years old? What major lifetime goals have you wanted to accomplish? If money were no object what would you do? If you had finished your college degree/had a Master's degree or Ph.D./had a different degree or training, what could you be doing?

For some of you, this might be the only time you've allowed yourself to dream lately. You've been putting it on hold, telling yourself that that time would come later. Perhaps you haven't taken time to think about yourself in so long that you can't come up with any dreams. Maybe you're such a realist that you don't even want to think about anything that seems unattainable.

Fortunately, I believe that God not only allows, but encourages dreaming. Psalm 37:4 promises, "Delight yourself in the LORD and he will give you the desires of your heart." What a loaded phrase! Loaded with potential. Laden with anticipation. Lined with intimacy. Pray about those things. God already knows them, so turn them over to Him. Trust that He has good things in store for you and a tremendous plan for your life.

Write down at least three goals for every major area of your life: personal, spiritual, professional, marriage and family. For example, in my spiritual area, I might make a general goal of Scripture memorization. My specific goal would be five verses per week.

Under personal, I could list one hour of personal leisure time a week and the ever-present goal, lose the last eight pounds of post-baby fat. To accomplish them, I might agree to trade with my husband or another friend my hour for leisure. I could also agree to walk every night with my husband or meet a girlfriend for aerobics a few times a week. You get the idea.

Go ahead and commit a few of your plans to paper. As someone once said, "It's a dream until you write it down . . . then it's a goal." Make a one-year plan. A five-year plan. A list of lifetime goals. Now break each goal down into specific steps. Implement a plan to make at least one of them start happening. Today.

If you always wanted to be a lawyer, sign up for a class at a local college. Check into law schools, scholarships, and correspondence for general coursework. Subscribe to a related magazine. Think about taking a small step by getting a paralegal degree first. The important thing is that you do something toward making your goal a reality.

There are two other reasons that writing down your personal, professional, spiritual, marriage and family goals are a good idea. First of all, seeing your goals in black and white are motivating and convicting. It keeps you on track. You now have them and you know what they are. When someone asks you for a piece of your time, tell her you'll need some time to check your schedule and you'll get back with her.

Next, ask two questions: If I take on another commitment, how will this affect my family? Secondly, Does this help me accomplish one or more of my goals? If the answer needs to be "No," it isn't necessary to come up with a long explanation. Simply and politely say, "I'm sorry. Thank you so much for thinking of me, however it's not possible for me to take it on right now."

The other reason that the list is important is that you can look back on it and see how much you have accomplished and how God has answered your prayers. When I get discouraged I often refer to my list of lifetime goals.

I wanted to be a married mother of three little girls (I have four!). I wanted to be a high school history teacher, but I also wanted to stay home with my kids (I have the blessing of teaching half time: Constitutional Law, AP Government and American History). I wanted to be a writer (three of my books and several articles were published by the time I was thirty-five). I wanted a Master's degree (I finished my comprehensive exams and oral boards twenty-one days before my marriage to Greg!). I wanted to be able to share with people how very much God loves them (in addition to my writing I travel twice a month for eight months out of the year, speaking and singing at conferences and retreats). I wanted to go to Europe, Paris specifically. (I did get to go, in a way that I could never have imagined – see Chapter 10.)

Achieving dreams involves lots of praying, planning, ingenuity, and plain old hard work. But reviewing them and adding new ones always draws you back to the fact of God's faithful goodness.

Make a list of all the things you believed in before you were told they were impossible.
–Unknown

And then remember nothing is impossible with God!

Organization

"Finding balance" seems to be a popular buzzword these days. Experts tell us that if we can just figure out what and how much to do of everything we want to do, our lives will be wonderful. The longer I live, the more I think, "hogwash!" Trying for balance just makes me feel like I'm walking a tightrope with no spotters. It's the little, practical tips that have helped me the most.

QUICK ORGANIZATION TIPS FOR SMOOTH CHOCOLATE DAYS

- Pack lunches the night before.
- Pour cereal in bowls and put spoons and vitamins on the table, ready for the morning.
- When school begins, let each child pick out five outfits for the coming week on Sunday night. Morning dress time is hassle free.
- Sign permission slips, pack lunch money, book order money, etc., and place them in backpacks the night before. Have a specific place for each person to pick up his or her supplies on the way out the door.
- Put a hook for car keys and a tray or basket for outgoing mail and other small items that need to go with you, right by the door.

- Only touch your mail once. Open it by a wastebasket. Pitch the junk mail. File the bills. Answer the letters.
- Keep a "busy basket" in your car. Put cross-stitch, a Bible, notecards, and a book or magazine in it. Voila-something to do when you're stuck in traffic, waiting for the kids to get out of gymnastics/ball practice/school, bored at the doctor's office, etc. It's amazing what you can accomplish during these otherwise "wasted" blocks of time.
- When you begin a garage sale pile, put a price tag on each item before storing it.
- Place items for delivery to Goodwill or local charities in the trunk immediately. Next time you're in that area, you'll have everything with you.
- Make your bed first thing in the morning; no matter how crazy your day gets, there will be an oasis of calm.
- Apply the "10-second rule." Before you lay something down, ask yourself, "Do I have ten seconds to put this away?" Chances are you do.
- Studies show that we wear 20% of our clothes 80% of the time. Make a quick trip through your closet. Try things on. Have a garage sale. Swap things you're tired of with a friend's castoffs. Put some in a donation barrel.
- Try this for a New Year's resolution: go through every room of your house and eliminate four things. Less clutter means less of your life goes to cleaning.
- When you buy something new, get rid of something old unless the item purchased was to replace a worn-out version.
- Instead of procrastinating on jobs you hate to do, try these tricks: set the timer for 15 minutes and work on one task only until the timer goes off. Chances are you'll be so into it that you won't want to quit. Always tackle the biggest jobs when you're freshest. Save mindless chores like dusting or sorting for down time.
- Time yourself one day on how long it really takes to dust the house or vacuum it. Odds are good that when you see how comparatively little time it takes, you'll just do it and get it over with. Delegate some jobs to your children so they'll learn both new skills and the reality that being part of a family means helping out.
- Do a few chores each night so that your weekends are relaxing rather than cleaning marathons.
- Relax your standards.

- Don't cram free blocks of time with more activity. It's okay not only to pursue activities you enjoy, but also to do nothing! Mother and writer Katrina Kenison states, "If any event makes you wonder, 'How am I gonna pull this off?' It's too much."
- I have lots more tips in my books *PayDay: Treasures for Stay At Home Moms* (1998) and *The Welcome Place: Porch Swings & Picnics* (to be released).

If you believe national statistics, a good place to begin eliminating things that waste time would be what one comedian dubbed, "Must flee TV." On average, Americans watch more than three hours of TV a day! At twenty-one hours per week, that would give us nearly an extra day every week! Think of what you could do with that kind of time.

ENJOYING CHOCOLATE THINGS

- Just for today make a concerted effort to live in this moment. Don't worry about yesterday. Don't ponder tomorrow's "To-Do List."
- Take a nap during the next rainstorm.
- Have a watermelon seed-spitting contest. [When I was a little girl, my parents had the entire church over to our back yard for this event. The next summer we had a bumper crop of "accidental" melons!]
- Sit on the front porch steps and eat a popsicle.
- Make lemonade from scratch.
- Hang wind chimes.
- Sleep with the windows open on a balmy autumn night.
- Put a note in your kids' lunch boxes and in your spouse's too!
- Buy a porch swing and put it up.
- Catch lightning bugs.
- Lie on a blanket and find shapes in the clouds.
- Walk barefoot.
- End every night by recording five things you've been thankful for in a gratitude journal. If you make it a habit, you'll soon find that five things aren't nearly enough.
- Start every day with this simple prayer: *Lord, thank you for the beauty of this day. Please let me make a difference in what I do today.*
- Choose one Scripture to meditate on every few days. Post a copy on your bathroom mirror, above the kitchen sink and on your car's dashboard. Memorize and incorporate those words

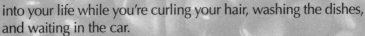

into your life while you're curling your hair, washing the dishes, and waiting in the car.
- Put a packet of potpourri under the car seat. It will release a wonderful smell on hot days.
- Have lunch outside.

In her fabulous book of collected quotes, *Wake-Up Calls*, former news show host, Joan Lunden, talks about an Internet quiz that really helped focus her priorities. Take it quickly.

- Name the 5 wealthiest people in the world.
- Name the last 5 winners of the Miss America contest.
- Name the last dozen Academy Award winners for Best Actor or Actress.
- Name the last decade's-worth of World Series Winners.

If you're like me, you had trouble coming up with more than one name. Luckily, the quiz didn't end there.

- List the teachers who aided your journey through school.
- Think of several people who have taught you something worthwhile.
- Name 3 friends who have helped you through a difficult time.
- Think of 5 people you enjoy spending time with.

I bet the second part of the quiz was easier. What a powerful lesson about how to prioritize our time. Spend it on people. It takes so little to make a difference in our families. In our communities. In our schools. In our churches. In our world. Bottom line: you don't so much get a life as you make a life.

It's been a good day. My husband gave me a great good-bye kiss when he left for work. I have written a little. Played a little. Talked with some friends. Read some. Run a few errands. Grabbed lunch with my girls. Gotten forty-five precious minutes to myself, combined with aerobic activity and a free tan while mowing some of the lawn. Rocked the baby. Changed a diaper and rocked her again. I just peeked in on my two sweet middle girls, snuggled together on their floor for naps. [Their sheets are in the dryer that is mercifully working!] Even as I write, my oldest daughter is curled up on the porch swing with Twinkies and pink lemonade, chattering animatedly and non-stop with a boy from down the road. He happened to drop by our house while riding his bike, because he knows I *always* have lemonade. And I'm starting to think that he may also think my oldest daughter is cute.

I'm not sure how I feel about that, but I am sure that being in the middle of all of these wonderful relationships that make up my life is the best thing I could possibly do with my time. Indeed, with my life.

Gaining a Chocolate Perspective

1. Read Jeremiah 29:11. Hands down, this is my favorite verse in the whole Bible!

   According to the verse, what are God's plans for you?

2. Psalm 31:15 says, "My times are in your hands." How does such knowledge comfort you? What impact does that have on your schedules, priorities, and dreams?

3. Read Psalm 90:12; Exodus 16:30 & 20:8; Joshua 1:8; Psalm 118:24; Luke 11:3; Acts 17:11; Philemon 6; and Proverbs 27:1. Jot down an insight from each verse about how we are to spend our time.

4. Ecclesiastes 3:1 assures us that there is a time for everything. Review the list that follows this verse in Chapter 3. Which things are present in your current season of life? Which things are you anticipating in the near future?

5. Hosea 10:12 admonishes, "For it is time to seek the LORD." What specific plans do you have for meeting with the Lord each day?

Bits of Chocolate for Personal Reflection

1. "The main thing is to keep the main thing the main thing," Stephen Covey. Scripture puts it another way, "Where your treasure is, there your heart will be also" (Matthew 6:21).

   Is there a disparity between what you say is the "main thing" in your life and what your schedule reflects? If so, what steps could you take to change this?

2. Get out your pie graphs and your concordance. Do a Biblical scavenger hunt and find a verse to correspond with each priority or task.

3. How would it change your life if you truly believed that the only thing that *really* belonged to you was time?

The average American woman runs 21 minutes late every day.

Hurray! I'm above average!

Chapter 8
Chocolate-Covered Varmints

"Cheerfulness is the atmosphere in which all things thrive."
–Johann Paul Friedrich Richter

He shot the first one (he was a police detective), clubbed the second to death with a shovel; and the third he killed with the weapon of choice – a garden hoe. What was my husband killing? Copperheads. Three of them, all in the same day, slithering on the grounds of our dilapidated, ninety-eight-year-old, soon-to-be dream house. And strangely enough, after the third one, I began to have compassion for them.

My fanciful imagination dreamed up scenarios: The first one was the Daddy Copperhead. He was scouting the food and sun situation for a picnic. (My alternate thought was that he was out hunting for his pregnant wife's latest craving.) When he didn't return, the Mother Copperhead panicked and went out looking for him. The third had to have been their adolescent son, finally allowed to stay home alone for the first time. A tragedy all around.

There are things in life, even chocolate-filled lives that are just downright irritating. What's worse is that it's not usually the huge tragedies that bog us down. It's the "little foxes that spoil the vineyard." The daily irritants rub against our souls until we get a raw, tender blister and eventually a hard callous.

Difficult People

Like those copperheads, there are people whose markings we can't see until we get too close to them. In the right environment they can even be helpful; when we meet them unprepared, they can be dangerous. Chances are you know one. I sure do, and in my efforts to get along with them, I've come up with six rules for dealing compassionately with copperheads.

1. Meet them on their level – It was our oldest daughter Eden (she was 9, need I say more?) who noticed the first snake. She was squatting in front of it, pointing excitedly and yelling. "Daddy, Daddy! Look! A real live snake! I've never seen one this close before!" Before his booming voice put the fear of snakes into her, she was marveling at the artistic markings on the snake's back and admiring the quick darting of that forked tongue.

Just as we get down on our knees to comfort, soothe, or relate to a toddler (no comparison to snakes intended) therefore meeting them on their own level, it is a similar gesture when we search out the perspectives and positives of a difficult person. We admire their markings, so to speak. When we take the time to notice what's important in a difficult person's life, we can gain empathy for him by understanding his point of view and what drives him. We might discover that only certain situations bring out the copperhead in that person. Or we find that she might just be going through a phase and her time spent in the reptile species will be short-lived.

2. Don't take everything personally – Those snakes weren't after us personally, they were just doing their snake jobs with their snake personalities. The same is true of difficult people. They don't usually target us as recipients of their bad moods or obnoxious behaviors; they're simply living life in their own skins.

I have a friend who never tells me that she's upset with me; she just makes sure I hear the news secondhand. This drives me nuts! I could take offense, but I learned that she hates confrontation. So lately I've started anticipating her concerns and assuring her that I welcome her comments. I also let her know that not telling me deprives me of the chance to make things right.

Next time you're "bitten" by a copperhead's sour remark or disgruntled by a real (or imagined) slight, take a moment to pull on their bootstraps, slide into their pumps, or lace up their Reeboks. A short walk in their shoes might help you see their perspective.

3. Maintain perspective – First, think: On the "big deal" scale, how big is this really? Compared to a terminal illness, the loss of a loved one, or even losing your job, whatever it is, is probably small potatoes. Second, instead of assuming the worst, try being optimistic. Think, *I bet Susan didn't ask me to join the book club because she knows I've been so busy lately.* Or, *Sam probably doesn't even realize that he hurt my feelings. I know how he gets when he's in work-mode.* After all, haven't you ever been brusque to someone in your rush to get things done? Haven't you simply forgotten a friend's birthday?

If you still feel hurt, you could go ahead and gently speak up. And sometimes the kindest thing we can do is gently jolt a momentary copperhead out of a martyr complex by helping him gain perspective. *Don't Sweat the Small Stuff* series author Richard Carlson writes of a time when he was whining to a friend about his overcommitted schedule, the errands he had to run, and the deadlines he had to meet. He fully expected his friend to commiserate with him. Instead, the friend's wry response put things in perspective: "Why should you be exempt from the rest of the human race?"

4. Recognize your own copperhead traits – At times there's a bit of copperhead in all of us. Maybe we hog the spotlight by bragging about our accomplishments or focusing only on what's going on in our own lives while conversing with a friend. Perhaps we've gotten self-absorbed and neglected a friendship until we need something from the person, or played the martyr in a tragedy of our own making. Maybe we've been rude to our family members during a hectic day.

When I was a child, my mother sang a song to my sister and me about "Herbert the Snail." The song told the story of a bunny whose gift of speed caused him to be extremely irritated by Herbert's snail pace. The chorus cautioned: "Have patience, have patience, don't be in such a hurry! When you get impatient, you only start to worry. Remember, remember that God is patient too, and think of all the times when others have to wait for you!"

That is particularly good for me to remember since many of my friends joke about running on "Cindy time." I'm nearly always ten minutes behind, so I've taken to telling prospective friends that if they can't accept that about me, then there's no point in us bonding! Recalling our own irritating traits can help us more readily extend grace to the copperheads we encounter.

5. Incorporate humor – Laughter defuses a multitude of situations. If it doesn't help the person you're dealing with, it often at least helps restore your own sense of balance.

Abraham Lincoln, well known for both his extraordinary presidency and his wit, often used humor to deflect copperheads. When he was a young lawyer in Illinois, he was once charged by a certain Major Hill with making derogatory remarks about Mrs. Hill.

Major Hill heaped abuse on Lincoln in front of several witnesses while Lincoln coolly kept his temper. Finally, when Lincoln had an opportunity to get a word in, he calmly replied, "I have always had the highest regard for Mrs. Hill and I never made any of the remarks you have attributed to me. Mrs. Hill is a fine woman and the only thing I know to her discredit is the fact that she is Major Hill's wife."

6. Pray for them, but avoid their hangouts – It is part of our calling as Christians to bring out the best in those around us. Our prayers can reach places we can't. Jesus set the example. We are to pray for our enemies, copperheads included!

However, while dealing with Copperheads is probably a fact of life, that doesn't mean we have to frequent their nests.

C.S. Lewis summarizes compassion for copperheads beautifully in his classic work, *Mere Christianity:*

> *The rule for all of us is perfectly simple.*
> *Do not waste time bothering whether you love your neighbor;*
> *act as if you did. . . .*
> *When you are behaving as if you loved someone,*
> *you will presently come to love him. . . .*
> *If you do him a good turn,*
> *you will find yourself disliking him less.*

"Love your neighbor as yourself," Jesus said. It gets easier every time you glimpse a tiny bit of copperhead in the mirror.

When Things Don't Go Our Way
"Blessed are the flexible,
for they shall not be bent out of shape."
–Unknown

One stifling evening, when the tedium of all five of us living in one room while we remodeled our ancient farmhouse, was losing its charm, we decided to escape. We opted for the coolness of the air-conditioned Pizza Hut and enthusiastically headed out.

Sitting down at our table, strapping one infant and one toddler into highchairs, we began sweating. Profusely. After we ordered a large half pepperoni/half cheese (your choices of toppings are so limited with small ones), we asked the waitress if she might turn down the air. "It's broken," she said, snapping her gum.

Figures.

On to the second grader's Open House night at school. After a successful and blissfully air-conditioned tour, we headed to McDonald's. "You know as hot as it is," whispered my husband conspiratorially, "Let's drive through and get a small ice-cream cone for everyone." I beamed, anticipating the frosty treat.

We got to the drive up window and my husband cheerfully ordered. "Five vanilla cones please." The order board speaker was silent for a moment.

"Uh, Sir? We don't have any ice-cream tonight."

"*Excuse* me?" queried my incredulous husband. "You don't have any ice-cream?"

"That's correct, Sir. We're, uumm, sort of out of it."

"No kidding," this under his breath. "Well, then, we won't have that, I guess." *Guess we won't have anything we want tonight,* was the pervasive mood in the car.

Sometimes, the simple fact is that life is not fair. As I mentioned earlier, Barbara Johnson puts it, "Sometimes it seems that rain falls on the just and the unjust, but chiefly on the just because the unjust are always stealing the just's umbrella!" We have a choice to make: Moan about the umbrella or enjoy the rain.

Sniffing crayons (one of the 20 most recognizable scents) has been shown to lower blood pressure.

Who Knew? *Things You Didn't Know About Things You Know Well*, Andrews McMeel, 2000

Traffic Violations and Poor Drivers

My own personal record is being stopped three times in seven weeks on the same street by the same officer. It's a long street. At mystifying intervals, the speed limit changes from 45 mph to 35 mph to 25 mph. Three stops by the same officer would be humiliating enough for any driver, but you have to remember that nearly all of the policemen know my husband. It's all I can do when they reach for my driver's license and murmur – "Dagnan. Hmmm . . . are you by any chance Greg's wife?" – not to lie through my teeth.

Before I married my husband, I was prone to irritation whenever I got pulled over. "How dare they? Why aren't they out doing something truly necessary, like arresting bad guys?" After looking at it through Greg's eyes, I now realize that I am the "bad guy" when I am breaking the law. Ouch.

One of the fastest growing safety hazards is road rage. In one instance, two mothers grew very angry when one of them cut the other off in traffic. The women exited off the same ramp. One of them got out of her car, exchanged heated words with, and then shot the other. You have to wonder if she didn't think that being five minutes later to her destination wouldn't have been better than the jail time that followed. At any rate, both families lost a mother in a senseless tragedy.

In a world where the realities of road rage and Columbine shootings are all too frequent, we owe it to our children (and the fellow inhabitants of this planet) to set a good example. It is imperative that we model and discuss constructive ways to deal with anger, hurt, and disappointment. It could literally mean the difference between sickness and health, life and death.

People Who Disappoint Us

Some of us are repeatedly drawn, like Charlie, to the Lucys of the world holding that illusive football. Time and time again we get ready to kick the ball and send it sailing, only to have it jerked out from beneath our foot, and it's we who are sailing instead. Landing on our backsides. As Lucy said in one of the *Peanuts* comic strips, "I like mankind. It's the people I can't stand."

Humiliation can be quickly replaced by bitterness and anger. My husband and I recently sat down with our girls to watch a special surprise movie that we had purchased for one of our family nights. *Larry Boy and the Angry EyeBrows*. Aside from the fact that the trademark Veggie Tales humor is enough to slay the parents as well as entertain the kids, the lesson is vital.

Unbeknownst to Bumblyburg's superhero, Larry Boy, an evil plot is afoot. Awful Alvin is plotting to saturate the citizens with angry eyebrows, and the beauty of the plan is that he won't have to do a thing. Awful Alvin grabs his sidekick "Lampy" (an office lamp, whom I think might actually be celery) and does a "villainous dance" to a disco tune.

"If someone holds on to their anger, my angry eyebrows can attach themselves to their forehead, and once they do, they'll be doomed to hang onto their anger forever!" Haaaaahhaaaahaaaa (evil laugh).

The climax of the film is also its theme: anger is self-defeating. Awful Alvin decides he wants Larry Boy to wear angry eyebrows too. "But," Larry Boy protests, "I'm not angry at anyone." Awful Alvin tries to get Larry hot under the collar. He puts a popsicle down the back of Larry Boy's supersuit. He blows a trumpet in his ear. And the crowning evil—he asks the angry eyebrows to fly off and fill up the Larrymobile with chocolate syrup.

Understandably, this makes Larry VERY angry as he contemplates the future condition of his leather seats. The angry eyebrows approach. But good prevails. "Awful Alvin," Larry Boy muses, "Sometimes you do awful things to me that make me feel really mad. But if I hold on to my anger, it has a hold on me, so I'm not going to stay mad at you!"

When the citizens of Bumblyburg see Larry Boy's courageous example, they, too, let go of their anger and their angry eyebrows fly away.

An unknown sage wisely observed that "holding resentment is like eating poison and then waiting for the other person to keel over." It is a fact that people will be unethical sometimes. They will hurt us, disappoint us, desert us. It is also a fact that we alone decide what our reaction will be.

"I don't have to attend every argument I'm invited to."

–Unknown

Dreams Deferred

Few things are as bitterly disappointing as feeling as though God has said "No" to a dream. Or perhaps, almost worse, the answer is "Wait." How difficult it is not to have things happen in our timing. It is tempting to give up. To scratch words like perseverance and determination from our respective dictionaries.

But then heartwarming inspiring stories come to our rescue. Over 80 publishers rejected Frank Baum's *Wizard of Oz* before it finally found acceptance. Danielle Steel wrote her first novel at 19; she didn't make the best-seller list for another fourteen years. James Dobson left his secure position as professor of pediatrics at a large California University for a two-room office in Colorado, to start a little something he called, "Focus On The Family." John Grisham carried his first novel, *A Time To Kill*, around the country in cardboard boxes in the trunk of his car, convincing bookstore buyers to purchase his legal thriller.

We remember that Hannah in 1 Samuel Chapter 1 was so discouraged about having children that the priest thought she was drunk when she sobbed while praying at the temple. Chapter 1:19 and 20 record the happy ending. "The LORD remembered [Hannah]. So in the course of time Hannah conceived and gave birth to a son. She

named him Samuel, saying, 'Because I asked the LORD for him.'"

What do we do with chronic setbacks? We try again anyway. As comedian Jonathan Winters said, "I couldn't wait for success so I went ahead without it!" We pray. We persevere. I once found this information in a frame shop, graced with the simple title, *"Perseverance."*

> *failed in business 22*
> *ran for legislature—defeated 23*
> *again failed in business 24*
> *elected to legislature 25*
> *sweetheart died 26*
> *had a nervous breakdown 27*
> *defeated for Speaker 29*
> *defeated for Elector 31*
> *defeated for Congress 34*
> *elected to Congress 37*
> *defeated for Congress 39*
> *defeated for Senate 46*
> *defeated for Vice-President 47*
> *defeated for Senate 49*
> *elected President of the United States 51*

The man whose life this list chronicles? Abraham Lincoln. A dream deferred, but dreams fulfilled too.

Even in his earlier defeats, Lincoln kept his trademark sense of humor and optimism tempered with realism. After he lost to Stephen Douglas during the 1858 Illinois Senate race, Lincoln was asked how he felt about it. He answered, "I feel somewhat like the boy in Kentucky who stubbed his toe while running to see his sweetheart. The boy said he was too big to cry, and far too badly hurt to laugh." By acknowledging his hurt yet refusing to quit, he kept the dream alive.

Telemarketers Who Call During Dinner

Vince Nestico of Detroit, Michigan, got fed up with the endless round of unsolicited phone calls. He began making up a humorous list of lines for telemarketers. I clipped and saved some of them, if for no other reason than to laugh (*Family Circle*, 5/9/00).

- I'm busy right now. Why don't you give me your home number and I'll call you back at my convenience?
- This isn't a good time for me right now. Could you call me back later when I'm not home?
- If the telemarketer asks if you are the head of the house, say: "No, but he's supposed to be back any minute, so I've gotta get out of here!"

One of my personal pet peeves is the Psychic Hot-Line calls. The phone rings and as soon as you pick up, a breathy recorded voice begins. *Hi. I'm Saundra from Psychic Advantage. I know you've been having time and money problems and have been waiting for my call. Call now for a free three-minute consultation!* Other than the obvious, my first concern is this: If they're so psychic, how come they don't realize I hate it when they call?

As I mentioned earlier, for help coping with this and other of life's small, petty annoyances I try and ask myself this question: On the big-deal scale, how big is this particular "varmint"? Will it matter in five years? In one year? In an hour? If the answer is no, the best thing I can do is often nothing. I don't need to slam down the phone. I don't need to honk my horn. I don't need to yell at my spouse. I don't need to stomp up the stairs. I don't need to lecture the children.

Indecision, Pettiness, & the Gimmees

Our minister tells the true story of a friend of his who was undecided on a course of action. So while driving down the road, he decided to lay out a Gideon-like fleece before the Lord. "Lord, if you want me to make this move, let me see a deer on the right-hand side of the road. If you think I should stay put, let me see a dog on the left-hand side of the road."

A few miles later, he saw a smashed skunk in the middle of the road. After contemplating the possible meanings of an animal that hadn't been on his prayer list, he determined that this was a direct sign from God – *Your attitude stinks!*

Maybe that's part of our problem these days. Writer Annie Dillard says this: "What could you say to a dying person that would not enrage by its triviality?" Applying that question to the petty things that rile us, we would have to acknowledge that not many of these little annoyances are worth the fuming attention we give them.

Think about some of them with me. PMS (one of the witty founders of the P31 Woman ministries calls this "Princess Must Scream" disorder!). Phrases that just don't match: act naturally; clearly misunderstood; pretty ugly; jumbo shrimp. Maxed-out schedules. Houses that won't stay clean. Not getting what you wish for.

Sometimes I get a really bad case of the gimmees. I see some picturesque destination on a magazine cover and I want to live there. I sit on a friend's new couch and I am instantly dissatisfied with my own. I look back at old photographs and wonder what in the world happened to me. Have you been there?

If it helps, *Good Housekeeping* published a "Happiness Report" (reported by Catherine Clifford) in September 2000. Money didn't increase the happiness meter by much as long as you have enough income to cover basic needs. Beauty and youth didn't help much either. Turns out life satisfaction remains fairly stable, regardless of age. Brains? Only a smidge of a boost in happiness. Good weather? Studies found that given a steady diet of pleasant sunny days, you take good weather for granted, so it loses most of its happiness factor.

Most people are born with a "a happiness set point," a level of joy at which they stay for most of our lives, says David Lykken, Ph.D., professor emeritus of psychology at the University of Minnesota. Getting a new house, new car, new wardrobe, or a dream vacation does raise our happiness meter—but only for about six months—then we're back to craving a new fix. (*Ladies'Home Journal*, Shana Aborn, 158, February, 2001). Along with the Apostle Paul, we desperately need to learn the secret of being contentment in any situation. The lesson? Little annoyances or not, life is pretty good, even without the wish list.

For little varmints, there are also sweet little solutions. A bouquet of flowers, for instance. Even if you have to buy them for yourself, a new study at Rutgers University showed that participants who received flowers were less depressed, anxious, and agitated for several days afterward. The study noted that it was not surprise flowers that mattered, just the flowers themselves. So go ahead and pick up a bouquet. A small but wonderful luxury.

Laughter. It reduces pain. That connection between emotions and physical well-being even has a scientific name—psychoneuroimmunology. It is known that laughter promotes recovery among terminally ill patients and patients recovering from surgery. It lowers infection and allergy rates, aids digestion and invites sleep. Laughter relaxes tension, strengthens the diaphragm, and is even said to help tone stomach muscles. It is also contagious. Steve Wilson, who organized the first meeting of the World USA Laughter Tour, in 1999, said that the purpose of laughter clubs is to "prevent illness and the hardening of attitudes."

I love practical jokes. In high school, I once conspired with a friend of mine from the youth group. We enlisted the help of other youth group members who all called the toll-free number on the TV screen. Our surprised youth minister ended up with 25 free copies of the *Book of Mormon!* I could share others with you, but you get the idea. Create reasons for laughter and pass them along to others.

It is also helpful to know how stress, even that introduced by varmints, affects your body. Stress releases the hormone cortisol, which may be responsible for those spreading hips! It only takes a fraction of a second for stress adrenaline to be released. The whole body is affected. Immediately vision sharpens, hearing improves, the thyroid accelerates, breathing becomes rapid and shallow, blood pressure rises, digestion slows, muscles tense, and our blood sugar levels rise. These changes are designed to protect us when they initiate the "fight or flight" response. When stress becomes chronic, however, it is harmful.

Prayer combined with humor and a healthy self-knowledge is another varmint cure. I once read this prayer, written by an anonymous pen, and immediately scribbled it down on the back of one of my bills.

Dear Lord:
So far today, God, I've done all right. I haven't gossiped,
I haven't lost my temper, haven't been greedy, grumpy,
nasty, selfish or over-indulgent.
I'm very thankful for that.
But in a few minutes, I'm going to get out of bed.
And from then on, I'm probably going to need a lot more help!
Amen.

Relax. It simply isn't possible to get everything done. (That statement isn't meant to freak you out; it's supposed to be liberating.) Besides, new research shows that exposing your children to a bit of household dust might actually protect them from developing asthma and some types of allergies. A healthy level of dust might even boost immune systems. One study worried that, with all of the anti-bacterial soaps and super cleansers that exist these days, we might be making our homes too germ free! Hallelujah! Release from superwoman cleaning guilt.

Anyway statistics show that every day, the average child swallows the amount of dirt you'd find on about eight kitchen-floor tiles; the average adult swallows the amount of dirt you'd find on one kitchen-floor tile. (Who does these studies?!?!) Just make sure it's chocolate-covered dirt (*Redbook*, Barbara Bailey Kelley, 192, 2000).

Pursue joy. Joanne Kaufman wrote about how simple it is to find joy with your children. She is preparing to serve lunch on the deck for her two children. Her six-year-old turns a devastating grin on her and asks the big question. "May we have soda with our lunch, please?" "This is a tough one," Kaufman writes. "So far, my children have perfect teeth, and I, whose mouth gleams with silver, do all I can to keep it that way. So: Cola or milk? Milk or cola? It's a beautiful day, they've both been good, I'm in a jolly mood . . . OK, sugar wins. Whereupon joy breaks out" (*Good Housekeeping*, 83, November, 2000).

Turns out my own moments of joy aren't so hard to come by. They happen every time my four-year-old comes running to me with any given object, explaining, "This is trainous [that's "dangerous," for the uninformed], mommy. It could sharp you!" It happens when my almost twelve-year-old, teetering on the edge of adolescence, sits down beside me for an unsolicited snuggle. It blossoms when my six-year-old sits on my lap and we guffaw together while reading the antics of Junie B. Jones. Joy creeps in the form of my freshly-turned-one-year daughter when she crawls to my knees and her voice sings in an upturned lilt, "Uh? Uh?" And what she's "requesting" is a spot on my lap to smother my face with kisses. It makes my heart soar when I hear all the girls giggling, playing, and getting along together. At such moments I would gladly stay in this time forever.

Don't worry about what you can't control. That eliminates most worry, in fact. My brother-in-law (who is a missionary in Taiwan, along with my sister and my three nieces and nephews) sends us family updates that often crack me up. He has such a good outlook on Taiwanese earthquakes, political shake-ups, and language struggles. I'd like to share part of his response to me after I had written an ALL CAPS terrified e-mail inquiring about a disturbing news story.

In email, etc. when you type in ALL CAPS it is YELLING. . . just thought you might like to know. No 1/2 of Taiwan is not so unhappy that they are burning things . . . however . . . yesterday and today were the 15th and 16th days of the lunar month, and on those days, people burn "god money" in bins outside their homes and businesses to appease spirits. Roughly about 95% of them . . . I don't know how many of them are mad, happy, sad, scared or queasy . . . I do know, however that of that percent who are burning things – 100% of them don't know the Lord.

We are fine and will let you know if we are not fine unless China attacks Taiwan with missiles, in which case you should probably assume that we are not OK, although there would be a small chance that at least some of us would at least be a little bit OK . . . unless the missiles are nuclear, in which case you can rest assured that we are 100% not OK . . . except that since we are Christians, we will actually be more OK than we have ever been since we will be with Jesus.

Then just to get my goat, he closed with this further tease.

It is now time to eat spaghetti and then we are going to teach English/Bible study at a nearby apartment complex. We do that every Tuesday at 7:30 p.m. . . unless there is a missile attack. Then we call around to see if we are meeting or not. Gotta run . . . just remembered that I am supposed to bring something to burn at class tonight.

I laughed. Hard. And then my perspective was restored.

And of course, chocolate. Chocolate stimulates the release of endorphins, located in the brain's pleasure centers. And it's pure pleasure to eat. Gwen Shamblin, founder of *The Weigh Down* workshops, was asked in an interview, "What surprises people about God?" she replied, "God loves brownies! He wouldn't have made the sugar molecule to fit exactly inside the tongue and send up a message of delight if that weren't true. God delights in giving us joy."

Although I never watched it, I heard all about the "Survivor" phenomenon. The story that intrigued me most was what some of one season's participants did for survival. They caught island critters of the small insect variety (varmints, if you will), cooked them and dipped them in chocolate.

I simply cannot think of a better way to swallow them down.

 ### Gaining a Chocolate Perspective

1. Read Ecclesiastes 2:1. Why does Solomon hate life? Have you ever felt that way?

2. Read Ecclesiastes 1:5-10. As negative as this seems, Solomon is teaching his readers an important lesson: our fulfillment cannot be

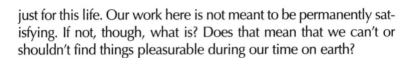

just for this life. Our work here is not meant to be permanently satisfying. If not, though, what is? Does that mean that we can't or shouldn't find things pleasurable during our time on earth?

3. Now flip over to Ecclesiastes 11:9-12:1-7. Why does Solomon want us to remember the Creator in the days of our youth? Many commentators believe that Solomon is urging us to live life to the fullest. Does such a suggestion contradict his assertion that life is meaningless?

4. Read Proverbs 19:3. Often, what is it that "ruins" our life? Whom do we usually blame? Why?

5. Read Romans 12:18. When might it not be possible for us to live at peace with "everyone"? What can/should we do in situations where that is the case? Can you think of any specific examples?

 ### Bits of Chocolate for Personal Reflection

1. Perhaps the most difficult aspect of life's little annoyances is the sense of being overwhelmed, of feeling unutterably weary. One of the things my Bible study requested of me this week was to rewrite the words of hope from Isaiah 40:28-31 as though God were speaking directly to me. I'll share with you my paraphrase, then I'd like you to write one of your own. Place it someplace where you can see it this week when a chocolate-covered varmint frustrates you.

Have you forgotten, Cinso?
I am everlasting, the Creator of all you can see
and all you cannot see.
I know you are weary, but I will never be.
I understand you better than you understand yourself.
I will give you the strength you need today and my power
when you feel weak.
Even when you were twenty, you grew worn out; burnt out;
stressed out;
trust in me only and I will renew your strength.
You will soar on Eagle wings.
Whether walking or running, you can make it without falling.

2. Read Psalm 132:1. Have you ever prayed a prayer like this? List a few hardships you have endured lately. Ask God for the strength to get through them and to bless you in spite of, or perhaps because of them.

Baker's One Bowl
"Death by Chocolate Cookie"
Found in the advertisements of nearly every women's magazine

- 2 pkg. (16 squares) semi-sweet chocolate, divided
- 3/4 cup firmly packed brown sugar
- 1/4 cup butter or margarine
- 2 eggs
- 1 tsp. vanilla
- 1/2 cup flour
- 1/4 tsp. baking powder
- 2 cups chopped nuts (optional)

Heat over to 350 degrees. Coarsely chop 8 squares of the chocolate; set aside. Microwave remaining 8 squares chocolate in large microwavable bowl (they put that in for the cooking-impaired like me) on HIGH 1-2 minutes. Stir until chocolate is melted and smooth. Stir in sugar, butter, eggs and vanilla. Stir in flour and baking powder. Stir in reserved chopped chocolate and nuts. Drop by 1/4 cupfuls onto ungreased cookie sheet. BAKE 12-13 minutes or until cookies are puffed and feel set to touch. Cool on cookie sheet 1 minute. Transfer to wire rack to cool completely. (Note: I much prefer to just eat them warm. It saves a lot of trouble) Makes about 1 1/2 dozen cookies.

Mary Rose,
Internet @ Atlanta
fans of clean jokes

Daily Exercise for the Non Athletic

*Listed below are exercises and
the calories they burn per hour.*

Beating around the bush
75 calories

Jumping to conclusions
100 calories

Throwing your weight around
(depending on your weight)
50-300 calories

Making mountains out of molehills
500 calories

Eating crow
25 calories

Bending over backwards
75 calories

Going over the edge
25 calories

Picking up the pieces after
350 calories

Chapter 9
Drowning In A Sea of Chocolate

People travel to wonder at the height of mountains,
at the huge waves of the sea,
at the long courses of rivers,
at the vast compass of the ocean,
at the circular motion of the stars; and they pass
by themselves without wondering.

–St. Augustine

"So, what do you want for your thirty-fifth birthday?" my mother asked. I've always loved it when she asks that question, because her gifts are always well planned and stunning. I didn't love it so much this year. It didn't help that I had just seen the OB nurse jotting down a notation on my chart at my prenatal check-up. Turns out it stood for Advanced Maternal Age.

"That's easy. I want the veins in the back of my right knee zapped and my teeth bleached."

Mother doubled over with laughter. "You too, huh?" She nodded in understanding.

"I'm only halfway joking, Mom. I'm sick of the kids using my leg to map out vacation routes and clothes aren't looking so great on me anymore." Then I thought about that statement. "They do, however, look much better on me than the alternative."

She smiled and settled on a bicycle as my gift for this birthday.

I don't remember how I learned to be critical of my body; I *do* remember when. It was in the seventh grade. Specifically in the girls' locker room at Parkway North Junior High School in St. Louis.

Every spring the school was required to give us a scholiosis test. Perhaps you remember? Pull your T-shirt up around your shoulders, drop your arms and bend waaaay over at the waist. Utter humiliation for a group of twelve-year-old girls. Out of consideration for the uh, underdeveloped, they herded us into two lines: Bras and No Bras. I was always in the latter line. But, oh, how I longed to be in the former!

On the playground, ornery boys would sing the birthday song to those of us who still didn't have need of even so much as a training bra. They closed with "Here's a pinch to grown an inch and you know where you need one!"

I was so over-joyed when my mother finally bought me a bra (do they make quadruple A?) that my friend Lisa and I wore our matching cream-colored Holly Hobby T-shirts and rode our bikes around the block, hoping the outline of our grown-up bra straps would be visible through the fabric!

It was no better in college; I still thought cleavage was simply cell division. I approached my wedding night with Greg in a state of trepidation. I told my girlfriends I was worried he might think my clothed self had been false advertising. When I lay down, one breast hid under each armpit! I finally decided to capitalize on what I *did* have-beautiful bone structure. He didn't seem to mind. Still my chest confidence wasn't exactly, er, lifting. After my first two daughters were born, I jokingly informed my husband that it would take another pregnancy to get me up to a C cup. Alas, nursing bras aren't exactly the ticket to beautifully showcasing any perceivable cleavage.

Occasionally I'd invite my baby-sister to go shopping with me. "Why?" she'd tease. "Are they having a sale on Barbie bras?" Just last year she e-mailed me from her home in Taiwan where she, her husband, and their three small children are missionaries.

"Cinso. Sure wish I knew your bra size in centimeters. They have beautiful bra and panty sets over here for cheap!" The only word I could see was "centimeters." "Ha! Ha!" I typed back. Turns out for once she wasn't giving me a hard time; in Taiwan they use the metric system for such items.

Studies show that self-esteem and healthy body image are still a big struggle for women. 76% of third grade girls are happy with their bodies compared with only 56% of seventh grade girls. Through Junior High well into adulthood, we are further bombarded with magazines whose images project perfectly sculpted women, who judging from the photographs, lead fulfilling lives in immaculate houses and have stunning relationships. Two words: air brushed. The women we see are basically illusions. Magazines use hair stylists, make-up artists, interior decorators, and even food stylists! We are striving to keep up with an unrealistic, unhealthy, unscriptural image.

A few days ago I received an invitation to a *Southern Living* party. A bunch of us girls giggled, ate great munchies and browsed through a catalog of household items that evoked warmth and welcome. A great time was had by all. But I recently read an article that made me think that perhaps *Pampered Chef*, *Tupperware*, and *Longaberger* parties might become passe. What's up next? You won't believe it! Botox beach parties and scalpel vacations. At the Botox bash, you could have your forehead wrinkles injected with the FDA approved derivative of botulism while sipping a soy milkshake. Sounds fun, huh?

The so-called "scalpel safaris" have eye or face-lift candidates traveling to South Africa for surgery; after healing for one week the newly tightened go an a safari. The article did warn however, that perhaps a safari isn't the best place to deal with any post-surgery complications (*Family Circle*, 15, 8/6/02).

When I speak to women's groups on this topic, I always bring a collection of magazine ads, taped to construction paper. We get a huge laugh out of one in particular. A woman in a black bra has her eyes closed and her head thrown back in delight, one hand covering her heart. [Evidently, this is one heck of a bra!] I show the ad and then ask the women if they have *ever* been so delighted with their appearance in a bra that they have struck such a pose from the sheer joy of it. The room is immediately filled with snorts and guffaws!

Reality check. The average woman is 5'4", 140 pounds, and wears a size 12-14. Yet the typical model is 5'9" and 110 pounds. That translates to a size 2-4! And they *still* feel the need to airbrush these ladies! Presto! No cellulite, no spider veins, no freckles, no wrinkles, and no red eyes, desperate for a good night's sleep.

Twenty years ago, models weighed only 8 percent less than the average woman; today they weigh 23 percent less! No wonder a recent study found that over 70% of women feel depressed and/or guilty after looking at fashion magazines!

Although we recognize this disparity with our heads, our emotions haven't caught up. Americans spend $34 billion on weight-loss products and services every year! A poll released by Bruskin Research for *Ladies' Home Journal* in November 2001 found that 71% of women think about their weight at least once a day. We constantly compare ourselves to magazine models and to the real-life women we meet. And somehow, sadly, many of us are left feeling inadequate.

I want you to realize something very important: Most of us are content with how we look and what we have *until we start comparing ourselves to others*. Did you catch that? Comparison starts the problem. Meditate on this for a moment. Ouch, huh?

That said, I do have to admit to my fair share of bad hair days and bad body days. My husband seems completely mystified by my ongoing dilemma between keeping my hair short and layered (I've worn it that way forever and I know it looks good) and my desire to grow it out so I can "do fun things with it" like whatever star in whatever recent movie I've seen. [Currently I believe it's Tea Leoni in *Family Man*. I finally got to see it on video.]

He is also out of the loop on the fact that the condition and behavior of my hair can sometimes make or break my mood. He is fascinated by the fact that I have, in his presence, apologized to strangers and grocery store clerks for the sad, sorry state of my hair. He is appalled that I will shamelessly take in a breath of awe and wonderment if I see anyone with good hair. Then I grab her arm and demand, "Where do you get your hair cut? I just loooove it!"

This doesn't bother me at all. I don't expect him to understand. When he has a bad hair day, he just throws on a baseball cap. Besides that method was precisely how I found my current hairstylist who is fabulous! (Thank you, Hailey!) I have been known to have a natural hair color attack or to ask for highlights to blend the gray. I am oblivious to the fact that my oldest daughter rolls her eyes at this. "Oh brother, mom. Now you look too young!" Is such a thing possible?

I celebrate the three good hair days I enjoy once every month. When Hailey cuts my hair, I ask her to spray it until it couldn't move in hurricane-force winds. Then I sleep sitting up. I am happy as a lark during these days. My mood is benevolent. I am the embodiment of the Mary Engelbreit sentiment, "It is good to be Queen!" Husband and children can always get a favorable response to nearly anything on a good hair day. Greg has gotten to where he rather looks forward to them.

And as for bad body days . . . I once read a magazine article that was advising women how to become comfortable with, indeed to love their bodies. This particular article suggested that we should stand in front of a mirror stark naked and pick out three things to admire. I laughed so hard I nearly threw up. I am the woman who wouldn't consider truck driving as a career because they have to stop at weigh stations. They could, I reasoned, subtract the amount of the cargo and truck and come up with my actual weight.

Being married to a police detective made it worse. There was no way I was going to tell the truth about my weight on my driver's license. Afterall, everyone pulling me over would be a friend of Greg's. My last two driver's licenses have happened to expire while I was hugely pregnant. Most recently at the renewal line, a sour-faced woman asked me for my weight. I mumbled a number. She raised her eyebrows in disbelief. "It's for the number before the pregnancy, or after the birth, however you want to look at it," I said defensively. I could've sworn she smirked.

Last summer at the public swimming facility, I was sitting with several friends on the edge of the pool. (Mercifully, I was five weeks postpartum and therefore exempt from parading around in expensive small colorful spandex in front of an unsuspecting public.) Glancing around, we saw tattoos, nose rings in belly buttons, and stretch marks in amazing variety.

The talk turned to analyzing this year's swimsuit crop. "Oh, look!" pointed one of my friends. "Panties with a matching rubberband!" "Ick," another sighed, disgusted. "Remember when thongs just used to mean shoes?"

Kristie, our petite blond Children's Minister's wife sighed contentedly. "Know what's great about swimming pools? It's so comforting to know that other people have cellulite."

No one seems to be immune from the problem either. When Julia Roberts posed for the publicity posters for the film *Pretty Woman*, it's reported she wasn't happy with her thighs, so she had them superimpose someone else's legs on the picture! Good grief! – we find ourselves thinking, If Julia Roberts isn't happy with her thighs, what chance do I have?!

A contemporary songwriter penned it this way: *"Well the straight-haired girls, they all want curls, and the brunettes wanna be blond . . . just as soon as I get what I want, I get unsatisfied."* Ain't that the truth? When we live our lives thinking that we'll be happy just as soon as we lose ten pounds, find the right mate, potty train our children, remodel the kitchen, buy that new dress, or change jobs, we are chronically dissatisfied.

We lose the ten pounds and find that gravity did something else to our bodies. We buy the new dress and then two weeks later, the cutest little sweater/pair of shoes/gorgeous coat goes on sale and we have to have those too. The kitchen is finally beautiful. So beautiful in fact, that it makes the dining room look positively shabby in comparison. We finally enroll in piano lessons and are so pleased with our progress. At a concert one evening, we hear someone else about our age who sings, plays the piano, and the tenor saxophone. Beautifully. Seemingly effortlessly. We fidget in our seats, envious. No longer content. And so it goes. On and on and on.

I kept a journal for my oldest daughter, Eden, from the time I found out I was pregnant until she was five years old. I recently read an entry dated a few weeks before she began pre-school. We were out on the porch swing and I was asking her what she thought pre-school would be like. She thought about it and then launched into a detailed scenario.

"I think the teacher will ask me, 'What's your long name?' and I will tell her, 'Eden Victoria.' And then she will say, 'Oh that's such a beautiful name! You color so pretty. Would you like to sit on my lap?'" Ah, such confidence! Most of us begin with it, but somewhere along the way, we lose it.

The more I research this subject and the longer I visit with women around the country, the more I am convinced that it's our perspective that must change. It is most certainly not wrong for us to want to look good, feel good, and be our best. However, the quest for perfection and our addiction to the comparison game is dangerous. Clearly, we're addicted. On average, women look at themselves in a mirror about six times a day. 52% make a habit of comparing themselves to other women to see how they measure up (*Family Circle*, 82, 10/9/01). The Psalmist wrote, "To all perfection I see a limit" (Psalm 119:96). Perhaps it's time we start seeing that same limit.

FUN CHOCOLATE APPEARANCE TIPS

- You already knew that curling your eyelashes makes eyes look bigger and more dramatic. Enhance that look by zapping your eyelash curler with a hairdryer for ten seconds. The heat will set the curl. Apply mascara as usual.
- Lightly dust sparkling powder across your chest, shoulders, and cheekbones for a bit of evening glamour.
- Pageant secrets: a dab of Vaseline on the tips of eyelashes help them shine and sparkle; a thin film of Vaseline on your upper teeth not only does the same job for an important evening out, but also prevents lips sticking to teeth if you'll be performing or attending a nerve-wracking evening event.
- Wear sheer, neutral hose or dark-textured hose with matching shoes for a long, leggy look.
- Invest in one pair of jeans and one dress or suit that fits you beautifully. When a bad body day strikes, go for this sure thing!
- If you have always been an advocate of the "tan fat looks better than pale fat" theory but wisely want to limit your sun exposure, try one of the new self-tanners. They're easy to use and are a great confidence booster. To keep wrinkles at bay, use sunscreen on your hands and face every single day, even during the winter months.

THE FOUR BEST (AND EASIEST) THINGS YOU
CAN DO TO LOOK AND FEEL YOUR BEST

- **Drink Water.** Research shows that water eliminates puffiness, banishes bloating, refreshes and hydrates skin. Additionally, it is thought that many of the signals our body reads as hunger are actually thirst signals. Drinking your eight glasses per day minimum just might curb the munchies. Best of all, it's non-caloric and free! [For extra sparkle add a lemon slice or lime wedge to your water.]

- **Get enough sleep.** I know, I know. But seriously, no amount of make-up or clothing can hide what sleep loss does to your face and temperament. How serious is this? Some studies say that sleep deprivation can cause a reaction time nearly as slowed as that when alcohol is present in your system! Current estimates are that 30% of adults are short on sleep by two hours per night. Start by guarding eight hours of sleep a night. You can decrease or increase that amount by fifteen-minute increments to see what your ideal sleep time is. You should be able to awake easily and feel refreshed. If you're a mother with an infant, sleep when he sleeps. The dirty house will still be there when you wake up. Or next week, whichever comes first. You should also note that sleep specialists feel that every hour of sleep *before* midnight is roughly equal to two hours of sleep after midnight. The message? Turn in as early as you can.

- **Do at least some exercise.** The good news is that a loss of just five pounds makes a difference in how hard your heart has to work. Three 10-minute intervals of aerobic activity throughout the day have the same aerobic benefits as one concentrated session. Firm, toned skin looks better and therefore makes you feel better, no matter what your weight. Don't be obsessed with numbers – judge by how your clothes fit and how much energy you have.

- **Incorporate leisure into your routine.** In February 2001, CNN news reported on an Oxford Health study. One in five don't take vacations. 18% say it's because they have "too much work." 32% of workers eat lunch and work at the same time. Yet a University of Pittsburgh study found that men who take the time for an annual vacation were 32% less likely to die of coronary disease. Block out some time for yourself each day. You schedule everything else that is important; this is too. Read a book. Take a long bath. Do something that energizes or refreshes you. It makes you a better partner, worker, parent, and friend.

Finally, take a lesson from the men. They have the right idea. A few years ago, the girls and I accompanied Greg to a business conference in Scottsdale, Arizona. While he was in seminars all day, we slept in, ate a wonderful complimentary breakfast buffet and then lounged poolside. I made a striking discovery. While I felt a mite uncomfortable parading around in my modest swimsuit after having consumed seven blueberry pancakes, evidently I wasn't alone. The women left on cover-ups, draped themselves at strategically odd angles over lawn furniture, or stayed standing, trying to present their bodies at the best angle.

It was the men, however, who fascinated me. Whether they were buff enough for the cover of a body building mag, or had stomachs with enough overhang to provide shade for myself and the children, they strutted around the pool with confidence. They swam boldly. They didn't walk around with their hands folded over their mid-section. They flirted. They made eye contact with anyone and everyone. In fact, I daresay many of them were preening. Research backs me up. According to a recent Gallup poll only 19% of men don't like their bodies; a mere 17% wish they were more attractive.

Need further proof ? Check out info from this Associated Press article. "Disco Ernie" is an 86-year-old man from Terre Haute, Indiana. He stands at 5-foot-5 and weighs only 115 pounds. He dances, sometimes as a male stripper, for bachelorette parties, birthday parties, or "embarrass your co-worker" parties. Now, don't get me wrong, I'm not advocating building self-esteem by stripping (as if!), just pointing out that positive body image certainly doesn't depend on appearance.

One man, R.G. Daniels had this to say about being hair-challenged. "The most delightful advantage of being bald – one can actually hear snowflakes." Perhaps there's a lesson there too. Less comparisons, more gratitude. Petition magazines to start using real live women for their covers; no airbrushing allowed. Maybe we could practice contentment marketing; I know there's a need for it.

Let's not forget that we are made in *His* image. How dreadful could that be? Psalm 139:14 reminds us that we are fearfully and wonderfully made. Next time you're tempted to be negative about your appearance or abilities try hearing those bald-headed snowflakes with your perspective. Catch them in a bowl and top them with chocolate sprinkles.

"Be careful reading health books, you might die of a misprint."
–Mark Twain

Gaining a Chocolate Perspective

1. Read 1 Samuel 16:7. What does man judge someone by? By contrast, how does God judge? Why do you think we are so prone to look at a person's exterior packaging?

2. Read Galatians 2:6 and John 7:24. How can judging by outward appearance impair a "right judgment"?

3. According to 1 Peter 3:3,4 how did women beautify themselves? Is Peter saying that it is wrong for us to enhance our physical appearance?

4. Matthew 6:28-30 reminds us that often what we find in nature has more splendor than anything we can artificially manufacture. Knowing this to be true, why do you think our worth hinges on what we can wear, or even what we can do?

5. Luke 12:22-24 advises us not to worry about our life, what we will eat; or about our bodies, what we will wear. According to those verses, why not worry? Go ahead and read 25 & 26. What can worry not do for us? Since it can't help us do this, what else does Jesus ask?

Bits of Chocolate for Personal Reflection

1. Has there ever been a time when you have made a judgment call based on someone's outward appearance only to have later been proven wrong? How did that make you feel?

2. Read 1 Peter 5:7. What parts of your appearance or your abilities worry you the most? Turn even that over to God today. Thank Him for the health, the body, and the talents that you enjoy.

New research from Cornell and Northwestern Universities found that people overestimated how much others would remember about them in situations both embarrassing and positive. Why then do we feel like everyone will shun us forever when we do something stupid or embarrassing? "The more focused we are on our own actions or appearance, the more we (inaccurately) expect others to be," says Thomas Gilovich, author of the study.

—Redbook, September 2001

Take the focus off self and do something for somebody else!

"If it can be verified, we don't need faith. . . .
Faith is for that which lies on the other side
of reason. Faith is what makes life bearable,
with all its tragedies and ambiguities
and sudden, startling joys."

–Madeleine L'Engle

Chapter 10
Broken Pieces of Chocolate

"There is nothing so bitter, that a patient mind cannot find some solace for it."

–Seneca

It should have been just another ordinary business trip. Like hundreds of others before. Kenny kissed his five-months pregnant wife good-bye and Julie waved him off with a contented laugh, a wish for luck on his presentation and an exaggerated thrust of her blossoming tummy.

He never came home. A freak accident cost him his life. A few weeks after his funeral, Julie also lost her twin babies. She came to my home seeking comfort. I held Julie's hands and the sleeping form of my month-old infant as she sat sobbing on my couch. "I can't do this. I can't stand it." My heart broke for her. We prayed together and I assured her that although I couldn't see a way either, I thought she *could* "do this." For through those tears I could see resilience. Something that told me she would come through this shining. I admired her courage and I told her so.

I believe what I said was "Jewels you are so brave. I could never in a million years cope with a world this broken with your strength and grace." A rash statement. It was viciously tested a short year later.

On a cold February day, my husband of three years, a minister, walked out on me and our sixteen-month-old daughter to pursue a homosexual lifestyle. Unsuspectingly, I entered our apartment to find $200 cash, a letter on the kitchen table, and a broken heart.

Within twenty-four hours, Eden and I were moved back into my parents' home. We lived there, trying to regain our balance for six months. My friend Jewels was one of many who rescued me in various ways. Fifteen months later and still grieving herself, she put me on a plane with her to Europe. *It will be good for both of us,* she begged. And it was her gift to me. My precious parents doted on Eden during the trip. For fourteen breathless days Julie and I toured London, Paris, Amsterdam, Munich, Austria, Florence, Rome. On the stone floor of a Roman hotel we sat and cried, pulling at scars, picking apart broken dreams, and gently stretching the hurt places of our souls.

We made a pact. Life would go on. We would pray for each other,

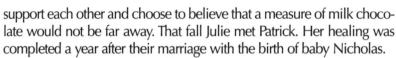

support each other and choose to believe that a measure of milk chocolate would not be far away. That fall Julie met Patrick. Her healing was completed a year after their marriage with the birth of baby Nicholas.

Meanwhile I secured a teaching job, back in the town of my college and courtship days. I marveled at God's timing and sense of humor.

Eden and I, just we two, carved out spaces of grace and a new life together and I slowly began to heal. Then came one of the darkest days. The day I sold my wedding rings and my wedding dress to pay the electric bill. What a mockery of things that were meant to be a legacy.

For three more years I was a single mother with new rules: No crying until after ten o'clock, so Eden wouldn't see. No letting anyone into my heart. Concentrate on my Master's program and my teaching. Go to church. Play with Eden. I wanted nothing else in my carefully re-constructed world. Bittersweet, long days indeed.

Eden and I spent time cuddled on the couch or on the porch swing each evening. As she grew, her questions and her faith, grew stronger. "Mommy, why don't I have a daddy who comes home every night for dinner like my friend does?" I did my best to explain. "I want a baby brother for Christmas." Again, I let her know gently, that wasn't a possibility. God prefers mommies and daddies to be married first. "Okay, then who can marry us?"

Feeling hopelessly inadequate, I explained to her the whole process of courtship, marriage, and building a family. I also told her that it might remain just the two of us and that would be okay too. God was our provider. She thought so too, because undaunted she replied, "Okay, then who can date us?" Her tiny three-year-old shoulders shrugged and she put her palms up in a puzzled gesture. Yet she was unwavering in her quest for a forever family. It became a part of her nightly prayers.

But let me finish this part of my dark chocolate story. God sent me the man of my dreams. One who is bound to me by a lifetime commitment to gut it out and by a thousand little nuances, habits, secrets, and shared experiences. He is the head of what Eden calls our "forever family."

When he gave me my engagement ring, he brought an engagement bracelet for her. Eden was beyond thrilled and told everyone (and I mean everyone) that we were getting married – all three of us! When my daddy asked her what she liked best about Greg, she replied, "Because he tells me he loves me!"

We reflected this answer to prayers in the wording of our wedding invitations:

For fulfilling my dreams,
for filling my life with magic,
for accepting my daughter,
for making us a forever family,
and for loving me without end . . .
I do . . .
Cindy Sigler Anderson
and
Gregory L. Dagnan
invite you to the celebration of their marriage
Saturday, the twenty-ninth of July
two o'clock in the afternoon

We made it part of our wedding. Eden and my Father walked me down the aisle. My daddy also officiated a part of the ceremony in which Greg repeated vows to Eden that he had written to her. He would be her daddy for life and he would stay with us always in this forever family. I responded with vows to affirm them in this endeavor. Eden beamed. I bawled. Oh, God is gracious! The closing song at our wedding was *"We're a Family."*

Our family added two more precious girls within three years – Emily Savannah and Elizabeth Grace. Our cup overflowed.

Then as is so often the case with life, dark chocolate ribbons intertwined and mingled with milk chocolate days. During my pregnancy with baby Ellie, cancer again began to wind itself around my precious daddy's spine and lymph system. It choked and threatened to strangle his life's breath. But he battled. He wanted to live life. And he wanted to wait for baby Ellie's arrival. He longed to hold her.

I made many trips back home to St. Louis, soaking up every moment we might have left. I wrote daddy a long letter of gratitude, thanking him for all of my growing-up memories and for the things he meant to me. My family made one more mad dash to St. Louis just three days before my due date. We wanted to savor the milk chocolate moments before the bittersweet came boiling out of the pot.

I sat on the edge of the bed and showed daddy the dress that yet unborn Elizabeth would wear when she came home from the hospital. He wrote in her baby book. *"Love you before I see you."* We read, sang, visited, and reminisced. How I hated to leave. I will never forget the look in his luminous, kind blue eyes the last time we told each other, *"Love you like crazy!"*

Three days later, baby Ellie arrived, squashed and surprised, screaming at the top of her lungs. I called mother and daddy, who was in the hospital by then, to tell them the news. I could hear the smile in daddy's voice, cutting through his pain and the phone lines. "Praise God! That's what I was waiting for! Now I can go Home." Twelve hours later, he died. He was fifty-six years young.

We made the trip home for the funeral with a four-day-old infant and heavy hearts. I held baby Ellie up to my daddy's casket (what an ugly word) so he could "see" her. The next morning we drove three more hours to the little country church in his hometown to bury him next to his parents.

Driving back down the gravel road knowing I'd never visit that precious country church or anything else with him again, was the hardest thing of all.

But I wouldn't have missed any of it for the world. The biggest tragedy would have been to have missed the chocolate side of life. To have left the box unwrapped. To have said of life, "I almost didn't go." We don't always get to choose our pieces, but the opportunity for this chocolate life is too splendid to leave unopened.

My daddy's philosophy was a good one. His motto at work was "Work is fun!" It was the same for life. When we girls were little, he was forever pointing out the "up" side of things. If we complained about having to walk from a far-away parking spot, he would admonish, "Oh, girls, it's a beautiful day! Be grateful you have healthy legs to walk!"

That attitude never changed. As the cancer made it increasingly clear that life was short, daddy penned these words in the last family letter to his seven brothers and sisters: "Life is fun. Life has been good to me." In the midst of suffering, he concentrated on the milk chocolate memories, and determined to squeeze the most out of every day. Just weeks before his death, he was out on our patio playing basketball, with my mother chasing after him, holding the bag for his morphine drip!

Do I miss him? Unbearably at times. Would I trade the experiences I had with him just to escape the pain? No way. God gave me a Father who modeled unconditional love for us girls, commitment to my mother and left me a legacy of strong faith.

A few months ago, Greg, the girls and I were watching a home video, the last one we'd sent to my parents before daddy's death. After making the tape, we hadn't watched it, so I'd forgotten the last scene. A VERY pregnant me, hands on my swollen belly, pleaded, "Daddy, hold on. Baby Ellie wants you to hold her!"

He never got that chance in the physical sense, but he has a hold on all of us. He was the one who taught everyone he knew to love the chocolate side of life. He introduced me to the One who invented chocolate and all the related moments. I don't think it's an accident that Ellie has inherited his same boisterous, glorious love of life. Sometimes she will sigh a big sigh and say, "I miss my Boppa!"

Even in the midst of sorrow, life intrudes. Mercifully, it goes on, even when we would rather not. There is still humor. Still the sun shines and the rain falls. Purchases are made. Decisions decided. Lessons learned.

One of my favorite tearooms serves a dessert called "Chocolate beyond Reason." It is part cookie crust, part mousse, and part cheesecake. It's every bit as wonderful as it sounds. I've been known to seek solace in a piece of it. But what gets me through the tough times with an even greater impact is the knowledge of a God Who Loves Me Beyond Reason. One who gave up His Son, One who hold every moment of my days, One who loves me without end.

Sometimes we need milk chocolate superimposed onto dark chocolate so we can survive. We like to be let down easy.

A twin once asked his brother to keep his cat for him while he went on an extended vacation to Europe. He called to check on his pet during the trip and his brother had some bad news for him.

The beloved cat had fallen out of a tree and died.

"I can't believe you just told me that!" lamented the brother. "You shouldn't just announce something like that so bluntly."

"What *should* I have said?" asked his bewildered twin.

"Oh, break it to me gently. Something like: Fluffy was up on the roof and I got a ladder and tried to go get him. Then he jumped in the big oak tree and I called firefighters and they're working to get him down.

"The next time I called, you could continue. Fluffy fell, and despite heroic efforts, he had to go to the vet. They're giving him man to cat resuscitation and a couple of shots. He might not make it . . . and so on."

Lesson duly noted, the twin was ready the next time his brother called.

"How's mom?"

"Well," he replied, "Mom was up on the roof and. . . ."

Indeed sometimes chocolate comes tumbling out of the box shattered. No longer whole. We do the best we can, scooping up the pieces and putting them back. Sometimes chocolate has had a rough ride to its destination. The box has been dropped, torn, crushed.

Dark chocolate days simply make the milk chocolate days all the sweeter. We could not appreciate the peals of laughter without sober silence. Health without pain. Companionship without loneliness. Holding without loss. Color without darkness. Being sated without having been empty.

Job's story continues to amaze me. From the first chapter, I'm hooked. A messenger comes to Job and reports that his livestock were grazing and some Sabeans swooped down and stole them all and killed all his servants except this one. *While he was still speaking* (verse 16) someone else comes to report that all his sheep and servants were burned when God's fire fell from the sky and he's the only one left to tell about. *While he was still speaking* (verse 17) yet another messenger came. "The Chaldeans formed three raiding parties and carried off all the camels and killed all the servants tending them, except me!" *While he was still speaking* (verse 18) one final messenger delivers the clincher: a mighty wind collapsed the roof on Job's oldest son's house, killing all of Job's children! All of them! Just think of it!

And if all these disasters aren't enough, Chapter 2 announces that God gave Satan permission to test Job up to the requirement of his life. Satan afflicted Job with "painful sores from the soles of his feet to the top of his head" (verse 6). To top it off, his wife sniped, "Are you still holding on to your integrity? Curse God and die!" (verse 9). (Kind of makes you wonder why she wasn't the one in the house with the strong wind instead of the children, huh?) Job's three friends, who go to him with the intent of sympathizing and comforting him, don't say anything for an entire week because they can see how great his suffering is. When they do start talking, they forget their original intent and wax philosophical instead. There is a technical term for how that makes you feel. Yucky.

Don't you just hate it when people minimize your pain? You share with a friend about your terrible day and she replies, "Oh yeah? That's nothing compared with my day. . . ."

You miscarry the precious life growing inside you and someone says, "Be thankful for the children you've got," or "You're young, you can always have another one." As though they're replaceable.

Your mate has died and at the funeral, some well-meaning soul reminds, "At least he's not suffering. He's in a better place." True, but how deep the obscenity of one plate, one cup, one fork at dinner. Of a bed that only has need of a single pillow.

You suffer from infertility. Your colleagues just remind you how good you've got it. There's no one to mess up that gorgeous new house you bought [never mind that the extra room you'd planned for a nursery shouts with emptiness] and you get a full night's sleep every night [how you'd love to have a warm bundle to rock in the middle of that night].

You're still single and share with a group of married friends about your desire for a soulmate. Laughingly, they tease, "Yes, but you're so unencumbered! Just enjoy it!"

Blessedly, Job's story doesn't end like it began. After thirty-seven chapters of silence, God spoke. "Who is this that darkens my counsel with words without knowledge? Brace yourself like a man; I will question you and you shall answer me" (Job 38:2,3). God asks Job if he understands the universe. Was he there when the foundations for the world were laid? Is he able to change the seasons? Does the eagle soar at Job's command?

Of course not. God does not answer Job like this to be cruel. In his wisdom, He does three things. First, He leaves us this record so we know that a God who is not big enough for tough questions is not big enough to be God. Second, in His infinite tenderness, He reminds us that even if He explained, we wouldn't understand. Not right now. His timing is not ours; His ways are not ours.

Lastly, He ends Job's testing by blessing him more in the last half of his life than in the first (Job 42:10-17). The message? Take heart. Have hope. We know the end of the story. Jesus came. He died. He rose. He's coming again, and this time, we will dwell with Him forever. No more sickness, no more sorrow, no more pain. No more dark chocolate.

Meanwhile, the Hebrew writer assures us that "we do not have a high priest who is unable to sympathize with out weaknesses. . . . Let us then approach the throne of grace with confidence, so that we may receive mercy and find grace to help us in our time of need" (Hebrews 4:15, 16). He knows, He cares, and even better, He can do something about it! Like giving us access to the throne of God Himself, no middleman necessary!

In the midst of her experience with dark, broken chocolate, Harriet Beecher Stowe wrote, "When you get into a tight place and every-

thing goes against you until it seems that you cannot hold on for a minute longer, never give up then, for that is just the place and time that the tide will turn."

It's not possible to live life without experiencing dark chocolate, and I'm not sure we'd want to. Research shows that dark chocolate contains more healthy anti-oxidants than does milk chocolate. Its deep, rich taste apparently satisfies hunger for a longer time too.

I deliberately chose to share some painful, personal parts of my life with you in this book for two reasons. First, not for one moment do I want to minimize the pain and heartbreak of any situation that you might have come through or are still experiencing by blithely announcing, "Nothing to it! Just consider it chocolate!"

Second, I wanted you to know that my life has not been all milk chocolate moments. I never feel like someone has much credibility on the subject of pain if they've managed to bypass it. I want you to know that whatever comes your way, you can successfully overcome it. For I long to introduce you to, or to help you know more deeply, the King who endured the darkest chocolate of all: the utter abandonment of His Father *("My God, my God, why have you forsaken me?")* and the stinging reality of death.

But oh, the sweet ending. "Do not be afraid, for I know that you are looking for Jesus, who was crucified. He is not here; he has risen, *just as he said"* (Matthew 28:5,6, emphasis mine). Jesus understands our fears, our doubts, our pain. Not only understands it, but *experienced* it. Why? Simple. He loved you so much He died so you wouldn't have to live without Him.

Most of us have experienced our share of pain. Sometimes, what seems like more than our share. And if you haven't yet, you will. That's life. I'm willing to bet there isn't a person you'll meet who couldn't be utterly miserable if they chose to wallow in dark chocolate. But survivors don't wallow forever. They struggle back to their feet, licking the chocolate off their fingers as they go and they choose to concentrate on an indisputable fact: the backdrop of broken, dark chocolate serves to highlight the milky pieces. Infinitely lighter, infinitely sweeter, infinitely more treasured. Broken pieces of chocolate, after all, are still chocolate.

"Surely it was for my benefit that I suffered such anguish.
In your love you kept me from the pit of destruction."

–Isaiah 38:17

Gaining a Chocolate Perspective

1. Why does the account of Job's story end up being an encouraging, rather than discouraging story? Look at Job's laments in Chapter 3. Yet Job 1:22 assures us that "In all this, Job did not sin by charging God with wrongdoing." Does this mean that we cannot ask hard questions of God during our trials?

2. Job 2:10 says, "Shall we accept good from God, and not trouble?" Why is it easier to do just that?

3. Read Hebrews 12:11. What is discipline supposed to produce? What is the goal of discipline? When does this harvest of righteous ripe for the picking? At the time of discipline or after?

4. Read James 1:2-4. Compare it with Hebrews 12:11. How is this similar to the reasons we discipline our children?

Bits of Chocolate for Personal Reflection

1. What is the hardest question you have ever asked of God?

2. Do you think that deliberately choosing a positive outlook is the same as refusing to acknowledge that a particular trial or experience was difficult? Why or why not?

3. When is God's discipline the hardest for you to accept? Do you have a tendency to label every bad thing that happens to you as God's discipline, or do you realize that much of what happens to us is the result of living in a fallen world?

The smell center of our brains can identify as many as 10,000 different odors, one of which is chocolate!

"Happiness is not a state
to arrive at, but rather
a manner of traveling."

–Samuel Johnson

Chapter 11
The Trash Can

"Never eat more than you can lift."

—Miss Piggy

My daughter Emmy had just turned two a few days before we brought baby Ellie home from the hospital. Inevitably, they always send you home with a bottle of those stool softeners. Mine happened to be soft, translucent-red capsules. To put this in context, you need to know that we had to leave for St. Louis the next day for my daddy's funeral and move into a new home just twelve days after that. In all the confusion, Emmy somehow managed to open the childproof bottle of stool softeners.

We finally realized this when we saw her on the floor, both hands scraping tiny bits of gummy red capsules out of her mouth and shrieking, "Not an M & N! Not an M & N!" Indeed not. We had been rewarding her attempts at using the "big girl potty" with M & Ms, which she dearly loved; obviously there was no comparison. We quickly called the poison control hotline. They told one hysterical mother and one bemused father that stool softeners weren't fatal, just soft. "You'll probably see some fun diapers!" the amused consultant chuckled.

It's rare for a chocolate lover, but sometimes it does happen. You open the selection of chocolate, bite into it, and it's just not what you wanted. You unobtrusively spit it out (or you make retching noises and fling it into the grass or out the car window) and then you're stuck. You've got the unfinished portion and the messed up wrapper.

You thought you married your dream man and it turns out he is glued to the remote. He can play basketball for hours but can't put a single sock in the hamper and even the mention of a trip to the mall makes him slightly winded. His idea of romance is a Clint Eastwood flick and a bag of Fritos with bean dip.

You wanted another baby desperately and after another round of fertility drugs, your period came. Again.

You believed in happily ever after and the divorce papers came on your tenth anniversary.

You went after that job or promotion with your whole heart and got your resume back with a form rejection letter.

You're widowed at sixty years of age. What will you do with your together dreams now that you're all alone?

You carried the child inside you for nine long months, tenderly watched him grow into toddlerhood, walked him to school, and now, in his adolescence, you feel like you're losing him.

That extra ten or twenty or . . . pounds doesn't seem to be going anywhere and there is absolutely NO Chocoholics Anonymous group at your place of employment, or even your town.

A close friend betrayed you. You shared your deepest soul secret with her, and now someone else knows.

You're addicted to the comparison game—marriages, possessions, bodies, lifestyles—and you never feel like you come out ahead.

That's life, precious friends and fellow chocolate lovers. It's *full* of wrappers!

Psalm 103 holds a beautiful promise in verse 4: "He redeems my life from the pit." At our best, Jesus Christ redeems us from a life that is *only* wrappers, without any meaning or purpose. At our worst, He rescues us from eternal death, the ultimate consequence of our sinful fallen nature without Him.

The opposite of living a redeemed life, full of chocolate possibilities, new every morning, is to wallow in the mire of foolishness. We are foolish if we respond to unwanted pieces of chocolate either by trying to accomplish wholeness without God or when we choose bitterness and self-pity.

This is not the life God wants for you and no matter how miserable we can feel at times, it isn't the life we want for ourselves either. First Corinthians 1:25 reminds us that "God's foolishness is wiser than man's wisdom."

When we make a deliberate choice to stop wallowing, then we are ready to lift the lid on the trash can, throw the garbage into its depths and allow God to create joy. T fashion beauty from ashes.

Though never easy to do, it's even harder when we realize a piece of our own choosing needs to hit the trash can. Then, more than ever, we need the assurance of grace. President George W. Bush expressed it succinctly during his presidential acceptance speech. "I believe in grace, because I have seen it; in peace because I have felt it; in forgiveness because I have needed it." Haven't we all?

Fortunately, God specializes in accomplishing what seems impossible. Even lifting us out of the stench of our own choices and using heart-rending experiences to make us whole again. His presence in our lives lights up the deepest, rankest garbage can. "People are like stained glass windows," wrote Elizabeth Kubler-Ross, author of the classic work, *On Death and Dying*, "they sparkle and shine when the sun is out, but when the darkness sets in, their true beauty is revealed only if there is a light within." That light can only come from one source. Jesus.

The condition of the heart is always reflected in our attitudes, our actions, and our faces. Be assured that I am not making light of your struggles. Often I forget and try to stuff some really putrid pieces of garbage back into my daily pack too. I am not talking about being deliriously happy all the time (although there are plenty of occasions for laughter, if you keep your eyes peeled); I am speaking of joy. Peace that transcends the situation. Calm that won't allow you to live under the circumstances, but above them.

Not too long ago I was at our women's Bible study on a Thursday afternoon. It's a special, marvelous group, with ages ranging from twenty-two to seventy-two. We were discussing the fruit of the Spirit and answering a question that was difficult for me at the time. Which of the Spirit's fruit are you most struggling to produce these days? The reason it was so hard for me to become transparent and share honestly is that I was struggling with, of all things, joy!

Hands down, that is always not only my favorite fruit, but also the easiest for me to produce in great quantities. For a few months though, it had been strangely, illusively absent. I surprised most of those women and myself when a single tear wove down my cheek as though it was on a waterslide in slow motion.

"Joy," I croaked, as though I were skulking about the back of an AA meeting. "I seem to be nearly joyless these days, and I'm not sure why. I've never had that problem before."

I was pulled tightly into the circle of their love. They prayed for me. One of them called me at home and pointed out that the anniversary of my beloved daddy's death was approaching. She reminded me that melancholy is okay and not permanent.

Another precious soul had obviously been thinking of me and praying for me, for at the next week's Bible study, she handed me a

note in her neat handwriting. "I found this last week in something I read and I just knew you could use it." She looked at me expectantly, the marks of time on her concerned face lit up with inner peace and a radiant smile.

"Oh, thank you, Anna! This is exactly what I needed. I am taping this to my steering wheel!" It's currently tucked inside my planner, paperclipped to a spot where I can refer to it whenever I need to.

> *Joyful is beyond happy.*
> *Happy is a quiet content.*
> *Joy, on the other hand is actively seeking moments*
> *when you're high on life,*
> *and if those moments aren't there,*
> *to make them. To cause them.*
>
> –Author unknown

That very week I determined to get to the root of my joylessness. I prayed. I talked over some lonely, deeply buried hurts with my best friend, who also happens to be my husband.

We prayed together that night, I healed some that night and pieces of that night's conversation will forever be stitched on the fabric of my heart. Joy began to return.

You've probably heard that the average child laughs some two hundred times per day. The typical adult? More like four. Sad, isn't it that we get so bogged down with our grown-up responsibilities and our ugly hurry sickness that we forget the whole concept of merriment. Of throwing back our heads and laughing aloud for the sheer joy of it.

Scripture speaks of the place for joy and yes, even laughter in our lives.

> *"A cheerful heart has a continual feast"*
>
> –Proverbs 15:15

> *"A cheerful heart is good medicine"*
>
> –Proverbs 17:22

> *"There is a time to weep and a time to laugh"*
>
> –Ecclesiastes 3:4

> *"Abraham fell face down; he laughed"*
>
> –Genesis 17:17
> *How I love the*
> *image this paints!*

"Our mouths were filled with laughter. . . ."
—Psalm 126:2

God does have a sense of humor. He has a way of disciplining with it, reveling in it, teaching with it. Remember Balaam's talking, stubborn donkey; Gideon's would-be army lapping like dogs from the creek; God giving the Israelites (after they whined and complained that they were bored of manna) so much quail that they were sick enough of it to vomit; God making senior citizens first-time parents; God sending a huge fish as thinking quarters for a disgruntled, runaway prophet.

To use the trash can for its intended purpose, we can't keep going back, opening the lid, and digging through the contents, looking for treasures. We have to be prepared for God to bury the garbage in the depths of the sea. God remembers nothing more about our garbage, once we surrender and ask His perfect forgiveness.

The Hebrews writer uses a different analogy. We are all running a race. We are to throw off "everything that hinders and the sin that so easily entangles" so we can run are race with perseverance. It would be awfully hard to run a race, much less win, dragging clanging cans filled with stinking garbage behind us.

One sultry evening I was forced to go digging through our outdoor garbage cans for some important trinket that the children thought had been accidentally thrown away. Because I love them, I ripped open plastic bags, pilfering through dirty diapers, rotten banana peels, greasy fast-food sacks, moldy cardboard juice containers and assorted slimy scraps from long-ago dinners. The combination of garbage and heat nearly made me gag.

Thinking about it later, I couldn't believe how willing I am to dig back through my life garbage. Rehashing old grudges. Leafing through the scrapbook of old sins. Replaying moments of incredible stupidity. Why would I do that when I have been delivered? Scripture promises that our sins, our mess-ups, our doubts, our struggles, our pain, and anything else that causes tears will someday be done away with. Forever. He will wipe every tear from our eyes.

Stop living like you still have to drag your garbage pails around with you everywhere you go. You don't. Resign from giving God control and then taking it back again, offering Him a list of suggestions as to how He might want to work things out in your life. Let go of the past. God is the God of second chances. Grab hold of your trash cans, pull them down the drive and leave them there. Permanently.

God will take care of the rest.

In fact, I invite you to revisit those carefree days of childhood and recapture the childlike spirit that God says we need in order to enter His Kingdom anyway. Your resignation letter might read something like this:

I am hereby officially rendering my resignation as an adult.
I have decided I would like to accept the responsibilities of an 8-year-old again.
I want to go to McDonald's and think that it's a four star restaurant.
I want to sail sticks across a fresh mud puddle and make a sidewalk with rocks.
I want to return to a time when life was simple; when all you knew were colors,
multiplication tables and nursery rhymes and that didn't bother you,
because you didn't know what you didn't know and you didn't care.
All you knew was to be happy because you were blissfully unaware
of all the things that should make you worried or upset.
I want to think the world is fair again, that everyone is honest and good.
I want to believe that anything is possible.
I want to be oblivious to the complexities of life and be overly
excited by the little things again. I want to live simple again.
I don't want my day to consist of computer crashes, mountains of paperwork,
depressing news, how to survive more days in the month than there is money
in the bank, doctor bills, gossip, illness and loss of loved ones.
I want to believe in the power of smiles, hugs, a kind word, truth, justice, peace,
dreams, the imagination, mankind and making angels in the snow.
So. . . here's my checkbook and my car-keys, my credit card bills
and my 401K statements.
I am officially resigning from adulthood. And if you want to discuss
this further, you'll have to catch me, cause. . . ."Tag! You're it!"

–Unknown

Now, does anybody want to come and play a game of dress-up Princess with me? I know the King personally!

Sound too far-fetched? Not really. "Cast all your cares upon him, for he cares for you." "Nothing is impossible with God." "Jesus Christ is the same yesterday, today and forever." "He does not treat us as our sins deserve." "I will restore to you the years which the locusts have eaten." "Do not be dismayed, for I am your God." "When you pass through the waters, I will be with you; and when you pass through the rivers, they will not sweep over you."

How rich are God's promises. Jeremiah wrote, "When your words came, I ate them; they were my joy and my heart's delight" (Jeremiah 15:16). Spend some time feeding on God's good chocolate words.

So, what's the secret? Get the most out of the chocolate that is life. Fold down each wrapper with care. If it's a milk chocolate moment, turn the wrapper inside out, stick out your tongue, and lap up all the remains. If it's not what you'd hoped for, crumple it into a tidy ball and toss it in the wastebasket.

Leave it there.

Move on to the next piece. For every dark chocolate candy, there will be another milk chocolate piece. I promise.

More importantly, so does God.

"God is so big He can cover the whole world with His love, and so small He can curl up inside your heart."

–June Masters Bacher

Gaining a Chocolate Perspective

1. Read 2 Corinthians 4:16-18. What do we look like outwardly compared to what is happening in our inner lives? What two adjectives does Paul use to describe our current troubles? What do our trials achieve for us?

2. Read Philippians 4:6,7. Do not be anxious about _____, but in _____, by _____ and petition, with _____, present your requests to God. And the _____ of God, which transcends all _____, will guard your _____ and your _____ in Christ Jesus. As you read through this verse, substitute the first two blanks with specific anxieties and praises. Also exchange the word "your" for your name.

3. The NIV Study Bible makes a potent observation about the above verses. "Anxiety and prayer are two great opposing forces in Christian experience. [Thanksgiving becomes] the antidote to worry (along with prayer and petition)." In what ways are worry and prayer at war? How often do you deliberately choose thankfulness as an option to worrying?

4. Hebrews 12:1, the writer speaks of throwing off "everything that hinders." What are those things? In verse 2, what did Jesus set before Him in order to be able to endure?

 ### Bits of Chocolate for Personal Reflection

1. I read this epitaph on a tombstone at the George Washington Carver museum grounds. "As you are now I once was; as I am now you will also be. Prepare in death to follow me." At first I found the sentiment to be chilling. As I thought about it some more, however, it seemed to be a message. People who have already died would remind us to live now. Our existence here is not forever. We have such a comparatively short time to make a difference. How does such knowledge change your thinking about garbage and trash cans?

2. Hebrews 12:27,28. What is it that cannot be shaken? Why does the Hebrews writer close the chapter with a reference to God as a consuming fire? Does that picture of God comfort you? Why are why not? If He is a consuming fire, then might He not also be able to burn up trash? [See also Matthew 3:12.]

3. Malachi 3:2,3 refers to a different aspect of God's fire-refining. What is the work of a refiner? How do you feel about being under the refining hand of God's fire?

Erma Bombeck's requested gravestone epitaph:
"Big deal! I'm used to dust!"

If someone says something unkind about me, it's important that I live so no one will think it's true.

If you leave things in the ironing pile long enough, you'll outgrow them!

Chapter 12

Choosing the Next Piece: Chocolate Souvenirs

"From a fallen tree, all make kindling."
—Spanish Proverb

What now? You've spit out the bittersweet remains, wadded up the wrapper and thrown them both in the trash can. But can you truly have milk chocolate again? Did your trust in God's absolute goodness vanish, or can it be restored?

The book of Romans is the ultimate read about starting a new life. It is full of joy and life lessons. Full of grace and common sense. It teaches us, of all things, to rejoice in our dark chocolate sufferings.

I don't know about you, but whenever a trial comes my way, be it an illness, a contract that fell through, or a terrible tragedy, my first reaction is to give thanks. I praise Him and can hardly wait to see what thing He will accomplish through it. [Wait! Go pick up the book from where you threw it across the room! I'm kidding! Sit back down and I'll explain. If you vomited on the book after reading that sentence, I'll wait for you to get a damp paper towel and clean it off.] I wish that were my reaction. It *should* be my reaction, but it's more like *Wow! I sure do love oversleeping. Thanks, God that you are making me a more patient person. Gee, thanks that I am in Kansas when I'm supposed to be twenty miles the opposite direction in another state and I'm late and I have no idea where I am! Thanks so much that I don't feel well today and I have a million things I'm supposed to be doing.*

Hardly the stuff prayers are made of. My sarcastic under-my-breath comments don't qualify as rejoicing in anybody's estimation.

Problem is, after God rescues me, I promptly forget all about it when the next inconvenience/dry spell/ sleepless night/ unbearable hurt occurs. I want to skip the suffering and perseverance part and get straight to hope. As for character, that's the word we use around this ninety-eight-year-old farmhouse every time something goes wrong. "Well, this house has such character!" And if you're from down South, then you're well acquainted with the phrase, "Oh, he's such a charuchter!"

Of course that's not the kind of character Paul is talking about at all. He's talking about what is formed in a person as a result of her responses to suffering. My favorite definition of character is *that which we are when nobody's looking*. What's our reaction to a person who rubs us the wrong way if no one else is around? How much do we give if we know it won't be appreciated? If someone won't notice? How hard do we work if we don't get an immediate and tangible reward? Do we fall apart in the face of the unexpected?

Best-selling mystery author Mary Higgins Clark became the widowed mother of five children at age thirty-five. She was also left without a life insurance policy because of her husband's pre-existing health condition. "Wringing my hands was not an option," she has said. "I had to get busy making a life as a single mom." She turned her dark chocolate into a writing career.

Pastor Ovall of Texas transformed a call from IRS Special Agent Struzik into a milk chocolate moment too. "Hello, Pastor Ovall?" Agent Struzik began. "I'm calling to inquire about a member of your congregation, a Dr. Shipe. Do you recognize the name?"

"Yes," Ovall replied. "He's a member of our congregation. How may I be of service?"

"Well, on last year's tax return, the doctor claimed that he made a sizable tax-deductible contribution to your church? Is that true?"

"I can have my bookkeeper verify it for you. What amount did he say he contributed?"

"Twenty-five thousand dollars," answered Agent Struzik. "Is it true?"

There was a long pause. "Tell you what, call me back tomorrow," replied the Pastor. "I'm sure it will be."

We don't get strong character or the hope behind it without persevering. Webster's dictionary defines perseverance as continuing a course of action, etc., *in spite of* difficulty, opposition. . . . (Emphasis mine). Take note of that important difference. We are to rejoice in our sufferings, despite them, not "because of" them. Paul's tone is too joyful to assume anything else.

Perseverance is well worth the effort. Often it is when we stubbornly dig in our heels, determine to trust God anyway, and just continue on, that we turn the corner on hope.

During my first few weeks as a newly single mom, back at my folks' house in St. Louis, I sat on the porch step every day, bawling and waiting for my parents to get back home. Eight hours might well have been an eternity. Man, I felt sorry for myself! I'm sure I was a pathetic sight to behold. After a while though, I determined to stop. I sent out resumes, I cleaned house, I started dinner. Eden and I took walks and cuddled. I exercised, I wrote letters. I read my Bible. I prayed, hard, for something good to come out of this mess. I did some detective work (a hilarious, if sad story for another book) and put together the pieces of why my husband had left.

I clearly remember the day that I knew I was going to survive. I had been halfway through my Master's program at Purdue University before my whirlwind move. My father reminded me that I would need to write and get a drop slip if I didn't want an "F" on my transcript for the class I was currently enrolled in. "No way!" I protested heatedly. "Daddy, I can't just quit! I'm nearly done with the class. I'm going to write and get permission to turn in my last test and my paper long distance." And I did. Every Friday I went to the library and forced myself to work, write, and study. I did finish the class and passed with a B+. More importantly, my character was strengthened and I knew positively that I had hope.

The equation Paul gives us is as simple as it is complex. Suffering + Perseverance = Character = Hope. "And hope does not disappoint us" (Romans 5:5). This is critical. We can hope all day long in an empty fantasy or a far-off someday that deep down we know has no hope of coming true. But this is different. Paul goes on to explain the reason hope does not disappoint us – *"because* God. . . ."* What has He done? He "has poured out his love into our hearts." Poured out. He lavished us with love. He gave the ultimate sacrifice. "Because God. . . ." No matter how you finish it, the point is that we cannot aspire to achieve our hopes, our dreams, or the lives we truly seek without God in the equation.

Romans 5:8 holds the key to understanding how very much He loves us. "But God demonstrates his own love for us in this: While we were *still* sinners, Christ died for us" (emphasis mine). It's so easy for someone to love us when we are dolled up, dressed up, and on our best behavior. We look lovable, we feel lovable. But the upkeep on such a front of perfection is not only impossible, it's exhausting!

How truly wonderful it is when someone loves us just as we are, warts and all. Agape love – love that embraces us *no matter what*. How miraculous when we remember that this Someone is God. When we finally come to this realization, life, no matter what our circumstances, is an occasion for joy. Sometimes, we just need to relax in His love, to stop struggling, stop telling God how we think His perfect will for us should be accomplished. Stop trying to fix things ourselves.

Often, just when it seems that it's just not possible for any good to come from a difficult situation, God surprises us beyond our wildest dreams. Genesis 18:1-15 records the wonderful story of Abraham and Sarah's unexpected visitors to their tent, one of whom was the Lord himself! Don't you know Sarah prayed for her bread to turn out perfectly as she prepared food for the visitors. It was during this visit that God affirmed His earlier promise that Abraham's offspring will be as plentiful as the dust of the earth (Genesis 13:16) and as numerous as the stars (Genesis 15:5). "At the appointed time next year, you and Sarah will have a son," said the Lord.

Imagine their skepticism mixed with cautious hope. Sarah laughed to herself. "After I am worn out and my master is old, will I now have this pleasure?" (Genesis 18:12). She has been scorned at family reunions for decades. The other women in town speculated about Sarah's childlessness. *Has she displeased God? Aren't she and Abraham having relations anymore?* She lived in a culture where a goodly part of a woman's worth was childbearing. Sarah was humiliated and discouraged. In Chapter sixteen, she took matters into her own hands. After living in Canaan (the Promised Land, remember?) for ten years with nary a diaper or descendent in sight, after having attended umpteen baby showers, always for somebody else's babies, Sarah was fed up. Her despair caused her to doubt God's promise.

Perhaps I misunderstood God. Afterall, the promise was to Abraham. Maybe the Lord really does just help those who help themselves. One evening after banking the fire and washing the dishes near the well, she beckoned Abraham into the tent. "The LORD has kept me from having children. Go, sleep with my maidservant [Hagar]; perhaps I can build a family through her" (Genesis 16:2).

Can you imagine the defeat and quiet desperation that must have driven her to make such an offer? The image of her husband sharing intimacy with another woman, and a servant, no less! The situation goes from bad to worse. "He slept with Hagar, and she conceived." Apparently, that's all it took. What a slap in Sarah's face!

What happened next was sadly predictable. "When she [Hagar] knew she was pregnant, she began to despise her mistress" (verse 4). Beyond irritated, Sarah blamed Abraham. He turned the tables. "Your servant is in your hands. Do with her whatever you think is best." So Sarah mistreated Hagar and Hagar fled with her son (verse 6). What a dark chocolate mess.

Yet here God is, showing up to remind them of His promise. He still plans to keep His word, even after their failed attempts to fix the situation on their own. Over and over we read and experience the evidence of God's faithful goodness. Guess what? He is still good. All the time. He loves us despite our doubt, our struggles, our interference. And best of all, He still keeps His word. That alone is enough to make me agree with Julia Child when she says, "Life itself is the proper binge." And, it includes chocolate!

One of my favorite things about vacation is coming home. I love the anticipation of walking back into the familiar, another adventure under my belt and in my spirit. I develop my film with record speed and begin the process of pasting and recording new memories into yet another scrapbook.

I attach another sterling silver charm to my bracelet. A pinecone from Colorado's Mt. Evans, an orange from Florida, Cinderella's castle from Disney World, a log cabin from Silver Dollar City, all dangle next to the Eiffel Tower from Paris, the praying hands (my first charm ever), a miniature football, the state of Arizona etched with the Grand Canyon and the Arch from my hometown of St. Louis. Tiny trinkets, but they number among my favorite souvenirs.

They are reminders of precious memories. Of the fact that-after eighteen plus hours in a car with my family amidst sticky postcards and attraction brochures stuck to the floor mats, with a paste made of smashed banana peels and cracker crumbs, dirty diapers, thrown sippy cups, countless toys made annoying by the slow-motion sound of dwindling batteries and dozens of maps that will never fold in neat rectangles again-I will be up for this again next year!

Why? Because I have *chosen* to hang on to a souvenir. The aggravation, lumpy motel beds and boredom of playing the license plate game for the fiftieth time is eclipsed by the adventure. The exploration of new places. The shared experiences with my family. It's not unlike the post-childbirth experience. We don't forget the pain; we just focus on what the outcome was. We hold that priceless souvenir and all that work (they call it labor for a reason) seems incredibly worth it.

And so it is with life. It is worth the struggle; it births joy. For the true chocolate lover, (that is life lover) it doesn't really matter how the chocolate is served, whether it be on the most elegant crystal platter or straight from the paper wrapper, clutched in the sweaty palm of a toddler.

The Apostle Paul had this sense of balance between light and dark chocolate. Between seriousness and laughter. Between heartache and joy. Paul knew that you don't get one without the other. It's part of the deal. He wrote that he had learned the secret of being content in every situation. He appreciated the dichotomy of life.

He was balanced because he was focused on the BIG picture, realizing that God's name is *I Am*, not I Was. God holds our futures, and it is safe to walk into it with the One who has already been there.

As Christians we know this secret too. My daddy used to say that of the hundreds of funerals he'd performed, he'd never seen a hearse pulling a U-Haul! No, we can't take anything with us. The only time we have to make a difference is from today until our last day. And that length of time is fragile, fleeting, and uncertain. That means that the true point of the chocolate side of life is that we spend that life on the things that will outlast it. Think Godiva, not just Nestle!

Meanwhile, we know one sure thing – God desires the best for His children. In fact, Psalm 17:14 says of God, "You still the hunger of those you cherish. . . ." And sometimes I think He does the job with chocolate, both light and dark, that is the stuff of life.

And the God who gives us this chocolate? What a glorious reminder:

"He also made the stars."

–Genesis 1:16

Oh, my precious girlfriends – just imagine, the thrill of it all, this thing called life!

Gaining a
Chocolate Perspective

1. Genesis 18:14 records the Lord's query after He catches Sarah laughing at the prospect of being pregnant. "Is anything too hard for the LORD?" Do you think this is a rhetorical question? Why do

you think God asked it? Has there ever been one of God's promises that you have doubted?

2. Read the first part of Micah 6:8. In what ways has God showed you what is good?

3. After Job's incredible tragedies, read the wonderful words recorded in Job 42:10-17. List all of the things that Job was given after persevering through his trials. Ponder the phrase, *(Job) died, old and full of years.*

4. Which part of the equation in Romans 5 is most difficult for you to accept or understand? How does Hebrews 11:13 help you to put this equation in perspective?

5. Read Hebrews 11:1 and fill in the blanks. Now _____ is being _____ of what we _____ for and certain of what we do not _____. With this in mind, how might faith be the ultimate "souvenir"?

 ### Bits of Chocolate for Personal Reflection

1. Think of a time when you questioned God's goodness and your ability to salvage anything as valuable as a "souvenir" from that situation. What was the outcome? What promises or circumstances changed your mind? If you are still struggling, what insights from this chapter and the Scriptures in the study questions might help you?

2. What is one character trait that you really hope to develop in your life? How can your current circumstances help mold you and help promote that quality?

3. If you were to die tonight, what would your regrets be? How can you live tomorrow to eliminate those regrets?

> "In the long run the pessimist may be proved right, but the optimist has a better time on the trip."
> –Daniel L. Reardon

> "The cream of enjoyment in this life is always impromptu. The chance walk; the unexpected visit; the unpremeditated journey; the unsought conversation or acquaintance."
> –Fanny Fern

A Chocolate-Covered Book List
(in no particular order)

On Friendship
- Dee Brestin, *The Friendships of Women*
- Becky Freeman, *Real Magnolias*

On Marriage
- Dave & Claudia Arp, *The Ultimate Marriage Builder*
- James and Shirley Dobson, *Nightlight: A Devotional for Couples*
- Becky Freeman, *Marriage 9-1-1*
- Kevin Leman, *Making Sense of the Men in Your Life*
- _____, *Sex Begins in the Kitchen*
- Karen Scalf Linamen, *Pillow Talk*
- Stormie Omartian, *The Power of a Praying Wife*
- H. Norman Wright, *How to Encourage the Man in Your Life*

On Children & Family
- Cindy Sigler Dagnan, *Pay Day: Treasures for Stay-At-Home Moms*
- Becky Freeman and Ruthie Arnold, *Worms in My Tea and Other Mixed Blessings*
- Vickie Iovine, *The Girlfriends' Guide to Getting Your Groove Back*
- Katrina Kennison, *Mitten Strings for God*
- Stormie Omartian, *The Power of a Praying Parent*
- Susan Alexander Yates, *A House Full of Friends*

On God & Heaven
- Tony Campolo, *The Kingdom of God Is a Party*
- Cindy Sigler Dagnan, *The Lights of Home*
- Glaphré, *When the Pieces Don't Fit, God Makes the Difference*
- Max Lucado, *And the Angels Were Silent*

For Fun & Inspiration
- Philip Gulley, *Home to Harmony*
- Karen Scalf Linamen, *Just Hand over the Chocolate and No One Will Get Hurt*
- Joan Lunden, *Wake-Up Calls*

About the Author

Cindy Dagnan is a popular speaker at retreats, conferences, banquets, and marriage seminars. She is the wife of one remarkable man, and the mother of four small daughters. Her fifth book is under way.

She lives in an old farmhouse, where she writes, entertains, avoids dusting, reads, loves, plays and eats chocolate . . . not necessarily in that order.

She has written several articles for *Christian Standard* and *The Lookout*. Other books by Cindy include – *Scribbles: Sketches for Stressed-out Moms; Pay Day: Treasures for Stay-at-home Moms* (published by College Press Publishing); *The Lights of Home: Scenes of Home & Heaven* (published by Covenant Publishing). In addition to these, Cindy has written the study guides for Dave Stone's two books published by College Press, *I'd Rather See a Sermon* and *Friend or Foe?*